EVIDENCE GROWTH GUIDE

The JOSH McDOWELL TRUTH–ALIVE SERIES

EVIDENCE GROWTHGUIDE

Part III

THE TRUSTWORTHINESS OF

THE BIBLE

by Josh McDowell
with Dale E. Bellis

Published by
HERE'S LIFE PUBLISHERS, INC.
San Bernardino, California 92402

EVIDENCE GROWTH GUIDE
PART III: The Trustworthiness of the Bible

A Campus Crusade for Christ Book

Published by
HERE'S LIFE PUBLISHERS, INC.
P. O. Box 1576
San Bernardino, CA 92402

ISBN 0-86605-0205
HLP Product No. 40-268-5
©Copyright 1983 by Campus Crusade for Christ
Printed in the United States of America.

FOR MORE INFORMATION, WRITE:

L.I.F.E. – P. O. Box A399, Sydney South 2000, Australia
Campus Crusade for Christ of Canada – Box 368, Abbottsford, B.C., V25 4N9, Canada
Campus Crusade for Christ – 103 Friar Street, Reading RGI IEP, Berkshire, England
Campus Crusade for Christ – 28 Westmoreland St., Dublin 2, Ireland
Lay Institute for Evangelism – P. O. Box 8786, Auckland 3, New Zealand
Life Ministry – P. O. Box/Bus 91015, Auckland Park 2006, Republic of So. Africa
Campus Crusade for Christ, Int'l – Arrowhead Springs, San Bernardino, CA 92414, U.S.A.

Table of Contents

As You Begin

Why a Growth Guide?

Christians are often encouraged to believe the Bible, but with little regard to its trustworthiness. While I do not suggest for a moment the Bible is not trustworthy (I'll debate it anywhere), I believe it is critical to the vitality of your faith to substantiate the Bible's trustworthiness by adequate evidence. It is appropriate to check the credentials of a book that claims to speak for God.

In *Evidence Growth Guide, Part III* we will explore some reasons the Bible and its Author can be trusted. We will translate evidence for the trustworthiness of God and the Bible into practical Christian growth. *Evidence Growth Guide, Part III* is designed to give reasons for your faith and to relate those reasons to your everyday life and witness.

Consequently, I encourage you to view your study as much more than an academic exercise. Look for ways to apply what you learn to your daily walk with Christ. Share any insights you gain with your family, friends or study group. Permit God's truth to live through your life.

Put It to the Test

If the Word of God can be trusted (and it can), what tests establish that fact beyond a reasonable doubt? Both honest and dishonest skeptics question the authenticity and accuracy of the Bible. What answer do we give? I'm grateful that God has not left us in the dark. God has chosen to speak to us in a verifiably trustworthy way.

The Bible is a collection of ancient documents, some written nearly 4,000 years ago. More than that, the Bible claims to be a revelation of the infinite, personal God, Yahweh. So the Bible is more than an ancient document. It claims to be a revelation of God. But how do we know for sure?

We establish the trustworthiness of God and His Word in two ways. First, we determine the historic reliability of the document. Do we have a reliable record of what was originally written? Has it been safely transmitted to us? Does the Bible contain accurate reports of historical events?

Second, we understand, from the Bible, the kind of person God is. What qualifies a person to be trusted? Does God meet the criteria? What reason can I give for trusting God the way I do?

We cannot discuss the trustworthiness of the Bible apart from the qualifications of its author. A book is no more turstworthy than its author, and it bears the characteristics of the author. So the trustworthiness of God as a person and the trustworthiness of God's Word as a communication will be examined in *Evidence Growth Guide, Part III.*

God Encourages Scrutiny

Don't feel embarrassed or reluctant to put God and His Word to the test. God encourages inquiry. Jesus did not chide Thomas for demanding good evidence before he believed. Jesus offered His hands and side for examination. He gave Thomas adequate basis for his faith. He only rebuked Thomas for his predisposition *not* to believe (John 20:29).

There is a vast difference between seeking to discredit God's Word and seeking to know positive reasons God and the Bible are worthy of our trust. As you discover why God and His Word can be trusted, I encourage you to examine the evidence with an open heart and an inquiring mind. I believe you will experience a richer, deeper relationship with the Author of this trustworthy book, the Bible.

Be Prepared to Explore

The lessons in this Growth Guide follow a specific format that will help you discover God's truth. The only other book you will need is your Bible. Each lesson contains key Scripture passages to guide you on your exploratory journey into God's Word. We recommend you use the New American Standard Bible (NASB) in this study. The language in these lessons is personalized to encourage you to apply the truths to your own life.

Each lesson is divided into seven parts. Before you begin the first one, study the following thoroughly. You may also find it helpful to review this explanation as you begin the first few lessons. This will aid in fixing the parts firmly in your mind.

A Quick Look Back

With the exception of Lesson One, each lesson begins with a review of the previous lesson.

Key Truth

The primary truth dealt with in the lesson is crystallized, and the learning goals are clearly stated.

What Would You Say?

Interaction is the keystone of each lesson. Here you have an opportunity to stop, reflect, and reply to a common misconception expressed in conversational style. Consider the conversation to be personally addressed to you. How will you answer?

Let's Lay A Foundation

The core of each lesson consists of Bible study and basic instruction. Look up each Bible passage referred to and fill in the key words or analyze the passage for its meaning. As you progress through this part of your lesson, keep three major points in mind: (1) Consider. The questions sometimes draw from your present knowledge. Pause and respond to each one. It will motivate you to search God's Word. (2) Contemplate. Each lesson is designed to maximize your interaction with God's Word. Allow the Holy Spirit to teach you as you analyze His truth. (3) Comprehend. Be certain you understand the main point before moving on. These lessons are like building blocks. If you miss one of the first blocks, it will be very difficult to fit the others properly into place.

Feedback

Here is an opportunity to test your comprehension. Without referring to the material you have just covered, try to complete this section. The exercises are both enjoyable and informative. If at the close there are areas you don't recall, don't hesitate to turn to those portions of the lesson and review.

My Response

Here we share together how God applies the truth to our lives personally. There are three parts: (1) I share how God has made that truth meaningful to me. (2) You are given an opportunity to consider what areas of your life God wants to affect with the same truth. (3) A specific prayer of application summarizes what we have just learned. Identify with each expression and make it your own. Prayerfully consider how God can help you choose to make this true in your life.

For Further Reference

This section, included in most of the lessons, provides additional sources of information. It will give you the added advantage of reviewing the same material in different form. The books cited are available at your local Christian bookstore or can be obtained by contacting Here's Life Publishers, San Bernardino, CA 92402, (714) 886-7981.

What's Next?

Evidence Growth Guide, Part III: The Trustworthiness of the Bible is the last in this series of three growth guides. *Volume I: The Uniqueness of Christianity*, and *Volume II: The Uniqueness of the Bible* may be studied in sequence or as separate volumes. Each guide is complete in itself.

Some might expect a study on the trustworthiness of God and His Word to be nothing more than a recitation of dry facts. Nothing could be further from the truth! The vitality of our faith relates directly to the trustworthiness of God and His Word. It is our goal to delve deeply into the reasons why God's Word can be trusted.

THE BASIS OF OUR TRUST

The Objective

I enjoy antiques. Restoring "lost causes" is a family hobby that pulls us together, listening and talking with each other while completing a project. Dottie and I and the kids enjoy our 1932 Model A Roadster the most. Kelly, Sean, and Katie especially like the rumble seat. They think riding in the trunk is something new!

It took hard work to make our Model A roadworthy. I remember the safety inspection. It had to be outfitted with modern road equipment (headlights, turn signals, a license-plate holder) to pass the road test. I wasn't allowed to drive it on the highway until it met the safety requirements. I know my family is safe when we drive our Model A because I know the steps that were taken to make it a trustworthy car. I have firsthand knowledge of the repairs; I know that car inside and out.

To me, our Model A illustrates a spiritual truth: God can be trusted because he meets all the requirements. And, God submits to tests that verify His trustworthiness.

Knowing God in an intimate way is the key to trust. In order to trust God fully, I must know what He is like. The objective of *Evidence Growth Guide, Part III* is to acquaint you with the qualities from God's character that qualify Him to be trusted. We don't need great faith, we need faith in a great God.

Key Truth

God's authority, wisdom, power and control make Him worthy of our trust.

I will learn:

- what qualifies God to be trusted.
- that God's character is the basis for our trust.
- how God is completely capable of fulfilling His promises.

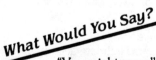

What Would You Say?

"You might as well face it; this is a dog-eat-dog world. Everyone is out to get everyone else. You can't trust anyone. In the last five years I've been ripped off by my business partner, sued for divorce, and swindled through a land investment deal. It's not an easy life – everybody lets you down. If you're going to make it in this world, you're going to have to watch out for Number One. Believe in yourself! It sure doesn't pay to believe in anybody else."

What would *you* say?

I would say _____

_____

_____

Because _____

_____

_____

———————————O———————————

Let's Lay A Foundation

Many ask, "Can we be certain the Bible is reliable?" The answers to those questions are found in the answer to a more fundamental question: "Can God be trusted?" Since the Bible claims to be from God, it can be trusted only as much as God Himself can be trusted. We need to find out if the God described in the Bible is the kind of person to be trusted.

I. The Bible confirms God's trustworthiness.

1. By declaration.

The Bible has a great deal to say about trust. One significant passage is an outright declaration of God's trustworthiness. Take time to copy the key phrases.

"For this reason I also suffer these things, but I am not ashamed; for

_____ and

_____ that _____

_____

_____" (2 Timothy 1:12).

Paul was not trusting in an ideology or a philosophy. Paul's trust was in a person – Jesus Christ. Paul's trust was based on his knowledge of what Christ was like.

Paul makes two declarations in this passage:
(1) His confident trust in Christ was based on his intimate acquaintance with Christ.
(2) His conviction that Christ was able to safeguard a trust was based on his intimate acquaintance with Christ.

One can rarely trust someone he doesn't know. That is true of our relationship with Christ. The more we know Him, the deeper our trust becomes. The deeper our trust, the more fully we know Him. It's a constant cycle.

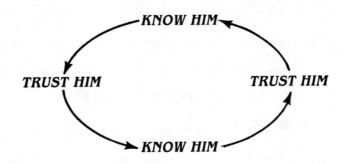

2. By invitation.

   Jesus invited his opponents to apply the acid test to His claims to be God. On what basis did Jesus urge people *not* to believe in Him?

   John 10:37 – _____

   _____

   _____

   What evidence did Jesus offer as sufficient basis to believe?

   John 10:38 – _____

   _____

   _____

   What would this kind of evidence enable someone to know?

   John 10:38 – _____

   _____

   _____

   In effect, Jesus said, "Trust me for what I do, not just for what I say." Words can always be disputed. Jesus backed up His words with His deeds, something beyond argument.

3. By investigation.

   Truth is always benefited by investigation. It can withstand scrutiny because truth has nothing to hide. The truthful man is never afraid of investigation. The Scriptures praise those who investigate the truth before accepting it. There is no gullible acceptance here; only open hearts and inquiring minds.

   What title was applied to the Bereans?

   Acts 17:11 – _____

What did they do to deserve such a reputation?

Acts 17:11 – _____

_____

_____

What was the result of their search?

Acts 17:12 – _____

_____

_____

Investigating reasons for faith does not create faith; it creates the atmosphere in which faith can thrive and mature.

II. The Bible reveals God's qualifications for trustworthiness.

Very few Christians can explain clearly what makes God worthy of our trust. In contrast, when the Bible asserts God's trustworthiness, it cites specific characteristics of God's nature qualifying Him to be trusted. Those characteristics fall into two categories.

1. Integrity.

God can be trusted because all His actions adhere to a moral standard of rightness. This is the meaning of God's righteousness: His actions always conform to God's character, the absolute standard of rightness.

When God made a promise to Abraham, what did God do to assure Abraham He would keep His Word?

Hebrews 6:13 – _____

Why is that significant? Why did He swear by Himself?

1. "Since He could _____" (vs. 13).

2. "God, desiring even more to show to the heirs of the promise the

_____" (vs. 17).

Take time to think through the meaning of this passage. What two unchangeable things symbolize the integrity of God's promise?

Hebrews 6:16-18 – _____

As if one were not enough, God removes all doubt about His integrity by offering two reasons to trust Him: the unchangeableness of His promise (He can't lie) and the unchangeableness of His nature (God is God).

2. Ability.

God's ability to fulfill His promises is set in the framework of His righteousness. He is able to do only what is right (2 Timothy 2:13). God has sufficient power and resources to accomplish His Word, consistent with His righteous nature.

Humanly, someone may make a promise, desire to fulfill it, and not be able because of extenuating circumstances. The reason may not be legitimate, but the promise is still unfulfilled.

God is totally trustworthy. He is able to overcome any obstacle to fulfill the promises He has made. In fact, through Jesus Christ, God has already overcome every obstacle to fulfilling His promises. In Christ, God's promises are a big "yes."

"For as _____ the _____

_____, in_____ they are_____;

wherefore also by   _____ is our_____

to the glory of God through us" (2 Corinthians 1:20).

God's promises are ready for the taking. What confidence we can have! Jesus is the yes to every promise God has made.

If Jesus had never come, we might have reason to doubt God's ability to keep His word; His promises might seem too good to be true. But a God who loves us so much that He gave His only Son is quite certain to fulfill every promise he ever made. Jesus Christ is God's personal guarantee that the greatest and the least of His promises are true.

God fulfills His promises through His Son because of four characteristics that make Him worthy of our complete trust. They are:

(1) Authority (total rights)

(2) Wisdom (entire knowledge)

(3) Power (sufficient ability)

(4) Control (complete rule)

III. The results of trusting God.

Many Old Testament characters illustrate the value of trusting God. We are taught the benefits of trusting God through their experiences. These accounts assure us that God always keeps His promises.

Solomon witnesses to God's faithfulness. How many promises did God fulfill?

1 Kings 8:56 – _____

There is value in specifically identifying what aspects of God's nature we are to trust. The experiences of Bible characters bear this out. They trusted God in at least four areas. When we trust God specifically, we see specific results.

(1)   Trusting in God's authority establishes my rights to His provisions.

(2)   Trusting in God's wisdom clarifies solutions to life's problems.

(3)   Trusting in God's power produces the motivation to do God's will.

(4)   Trusting in God's control determines my sense of purpose.

Conclusion

Since the Bible claims to come from God, we determine the trustworthiness of the Bible by determining God's trustworthiness. The Bible identifies at least four characteristics of God that qualify Him to be trusted: God's authority, wisdom, power and control. The more fully acquainted I am with God, the more confident my trust will be. That is borne out in the lives of many Old Testament characters. They were great men of faith because they were intimately acquainted with God. They knew what He was like. By specifically identifying those qualities of God that make Him worthy of trust, I am equipped to face life joyously.

A Summary of Our Study

The remaining part of our study is divided into three sections. Each section examines aspects of God's trustworthiness. In Section 1, "The Bible Can Be Trusted: Tests of Reliability," we will investigate the historic accuracy of the written documents of the Bible. In Section 2, "God Can Be Trusted: Qualifications of Trustworthiness," we will identify the qualities of God's character that make Him worthy of our trust. In Section 3, "God Can Be Trusted: Evidence of Trustworthiness," we will examine the lives of four Old Testament characters, substantiating the positive values produced in their lives from trusting God.

In each section we will learn something of what God is like. Therefore, from the consistency and accuracy of His written revelation (Section 1), to the qualities of His nature (Section 2), to the demonstration of His trustworthiness (Section 3), we will discover new insights into how to place our trust in God more fully. *Evidence Growth Guide, Part III* can be summarized in the following way:

THE BIBLE CAN BE TRUSTED: TESTS OF RELIABILITY	GOD CAN BE TRUSTED: QUALIFICATIONS FOR TRUSTWORTHINESS	GOD CAN BE TRUSTED: EVIDENCE OF TRUSTWORTHINESS	THE NATURE OF GOD
Bibliographical Test of the New	God is the Final Authority.	Abraham: Yielding to God's Authority	Final Authority
Bibliographical Test of the Old Testament	God Knows it All.	Daniel: Acknowledging God's Wisdom	Infinite Wisdom
Internal Evidence Test	God's Power Is Unlimited.	Gideon: Depending on God's Power	Ultimate Power
External Evidence Test	God Controls Everything.	Job: Submitting to God's Control	Absolute Control

Feedback

Without referring to the lesson, choose the correct answer to these questions. Compare your answers with the key at the end of the lesson.

Multiple choice

_____1. The Bible can be trusted as much as God is trusted because:
   A. The Bible claims to be from God. He is the ultimate author.
   B. The Bible is over 2,000 years old.
   C. God is a spiritual being.

_____2. God is uniquely qualified to be trusted because:
         A. His promises are recorded in the Bible.
         B. He is a God of perfect integrity and infinite ability.
         C. The Bible tells us to.

_____3. The value of specifically identifying the qualities of God's character we are to trust is that:
         A. We are instructed on the facts of Old Testament history.
         B. Trusting God specifically produces specific results.
         C. We are generally encouraged in our spiritual walk.

Respond to the following:

Fill-in

1. What four characteristics of God will this growth guide focus on?

   1._____

   2._____

   3._____

   4._____

—————————O—————————

My Response

Josh

I can't understand where she is – she promised to be here 10 minutes ago. I'm going to be late if she doesn't get here! I paced back and forth on the street corner waiting for my wife. Shortly, I saw her walking toward me. "Where have you been?" I asked. "I'm going to be late!"

In a calm voice she answered, "I was where I said I would be. You are waiting for me at the wrong corner."

I confess I often fail to give attention to details. My wife kept her promise; I simply didn't pay sufficient attention to the details to know how she was going to do it. That can happen in my relationship with God. He's never late, but I sometimes wait for Him on the wrong corner! He always keeps His promise, I just don't recognize it when I see it.

_____
(My name)

I am now able to identify the following characteristics of God that make Him worthy of my complete trust:

_____

_____

_____

As a result, the following is a new area of my life I will commit to Christ for safekeeping:

_____

To prepare me for the discovery of these truths, I will pray:

"Lord Jesus, thank You for being God. While I know You are trustworthy, I confess I don't know all the reasons why. I purpose to know You better, comprehending a little of Your greatness. I want to understand how trusting You affects my practical living. Thank you for this chance to know You better through Your Word. Amen."

For Further Reference

God invites investigation; He never asks us to believe blindly. Rather, God urges us to use our minds in trusting Him. Read, "Is It Sensible To Believe in Christianity or Is It Just a Matter of Wishful Thinking?" in *Answers to Tough Questions*, pp. 139-142.

Section 1

THE BIBLE CAN BE TRUSTED: TESTS OF RELIABILITY

BIBLIOGRAPHICAL TEST
OF THE NEW TESTAMENT

A Quick Look Back

I've discovered that trusting God's Word and trusting God Himself relate to the same question. I'm motivated to investigate the specific characteristics of God that qualify Him to be trusted. Most important, I've seen that the basis of my trust in Christ is how well I know Him. The more intimately I'm acquainted with Christ, the deeper my trust in Him will be.

———O———

Key Truth

The bibliographical test demonstrates that the New Testament text was accurately transmitted through the centuries.

I will learn:

- the key questions the bibliographical test resolves.
- how the bibliographical test establishes the reliability of the New Testament.
- how the New Testament compares with other ancient books in manuscript authority.

———O———

What Would You Say?

"Come on, be reasonable. Do you realize you're basing everything you believe on a 2,000-year-old religious book? A book *that* old can't be reliable! Especially a religious book! Why, the Bible has been altered and changed many times over the years. It's a simple matter of changing a story to make it more impressive. If you're basing your beliefs on an ancient religious book like the Bible, you're bound for disappointment!"

What would *you* say?

I would say _____

_____

_____

Because _____

_____

_____

———————————O———————————

Let's Lay A Foundation

For a moment, let's suspend our judgment on the historical reliability of the Bible and consider this proposition:

If God is to be trusted, the book that claims to reveal God must be trustworthy, a trustworthy God revealing Himself in a trustworthy way.

In this lesson we will examine the evidence for the trustworthiness of the New Testament – the first step in evaluating the Bible's historical accuracy and reliability.

In the study of ancient documents, three tests are used to determine historical accuracy and reliability: the bibliographical test, the internal evidence test, and the external evidence test. Those tests are cited by military historian C. Sanders as the three principles of historical research. I believe that the historical reliability of the Scripture should be tested by the same criteria as all other ancient books.

The bibliographical test examines the way an ancient document reaches us. Since the Bible was written so many years ago, can we be certain we have what was originally written? Since the original documents are gone, how can we be sure our Bibles contain what was written?

I. The criteria: time and quantity.

In the study of literature and ancient documents, the bibliographical test is useful in determining whether we have an uncorrupted copy of an original document. The bibliographical test evaluates ancient documents by two criteria:

1. CRITERION 1: *How much time separates the earliest manuscript from its original composition?*

    That criterion evaluates the interval between when a work was originally written and when its earliest surviving copy was made. The closer in time a copy is to the original document the greater its accuracy is generally assumed to be.

    Before the invention of the printing press, the Scriptures were transmitted and preserved through a system of copying and recopying. Before a manuscript became tattered and worn through age, a new manuscript was prepared from it. In that manner, scribes preserved God's Word accurately and readably. As centuries of copying and recopying manuscripts transpired, the potential of error increased. The bibliographical test provides a way to check up on the accurate transmission of those manuscripts.

    It might be visualized this way:

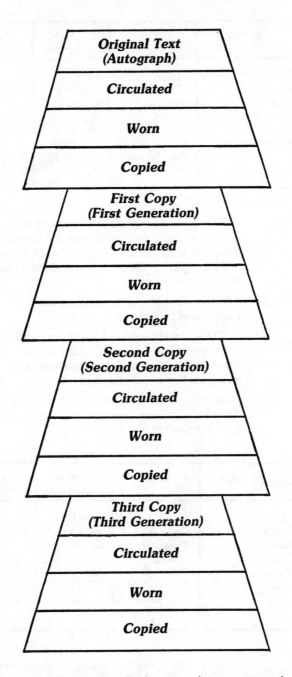

We start with the autograph, the original composition. As it decays, the first generation of copies is made. As generation 1 decays, generation 2 is made. Generation 1 becomes unusable, and generation 3 is made, using generation 2 as the model copy.

The question is, How far is the earliest known manuscript of the New Testament separated in time from its original autograph?

When we compare the New Testament documents with secular books of antiquity, the New Testament's credentials are astounding. Analyze the following chart. Which ancient book ranks number one according to criterion 1 of the bibliographical test? Assign them their ranks.

AUTHOR	TITLE	WHEN WRITTEN	EARLIEST COPY	TIME SPAN	RANK
Pliny the Younger	*History*	A.D.61-113	A.D. 850	750 yrs.	_____
Caesar	*Gallic Wars*	100-44 B.C.	A.D. 900	1000 yrs.	_____
Plato	*Tetralogies*	427-347 B.C.	A.D. 900	1200 yrs.	_____
Thucydides	*History*	460-400 B.C.	A.D. 900	1300 yrs.	_____
Homer	*Iliad*	900 B.C.	400 B.C.	500 yrs.	_____
Aristotle	*Ode to Poetics*	384-322 B.C.	A.D. 1100	1400 yrs.	_____
	New Testament	A.D. 48-90	A.D. 130	80 yrs.	_____

No serious scholar would ever question the authenticity of Plato's writings, despite a gap of 900 years from the original to the oldest surviving copy. When we compare the New Testament, the manuscript integrity is astounding! Hardly any basis exists for questioning the accurate transmission of the New Testament text.

2. CRITERION 2: *How many existing manuscripts are now available for examination and comparison?*

The second criterion of the bibliographical test examines the number of manuscripts that have survived through time. Scholars call them "extant" manuscripts. More manuscripts make it easier to reconstruct the autograph and locate any errors or discrepancies.

Again, compare the New Testament with secular works of antiquity. Assign each ancient book a rank. Give the book with the greatest extant manuscripts first place.

AUTHOR	TITLE	WHEN WRITTEN	EARLIEST COPY	TIME SPAN	RANK
Pliny the Younger	*History*	A.D.61-113	A.D. 850	7	_____
Caesar	*Gallic Wars*	100-44 B.C.	A.D. 900	10	_____
Plato	*Tetralogies*	427-347 B.C.	A.D. 900	7	_____
Thucydides	*History*	460-400 B.C.	A.D. 900	20	_____
Homer	*Iliad*	900 B.C.	400 B.C.	643	_____
Aristotle	*Ode to Poetics*	384-322 B.C.	A.D. 1100	49	_____
	New Testament	A.D. 48-90	A.D. 130	24,633	_____

The established text of ancient books comes from a network of manuscripts resembling a family tree. Several copies would be made from the original autograph, each serving as a model from which more manuscripts were copied. Soon, after several generations, there would be numerous branches of the manuscript's family tree, each branch bearing characteristic marks. By comparing them, we can easily determine which deviations from the norm are idiosyncrasies of the copies. If only one manuscript family survived of a particular work, the purity of that text would be legitimately questioned.

All that we know about Caesar and his Gallic Wars is contained in 10 manuscripts, the closest of which is a thousand years from the time Caesar wrote it. Yet no one seriously questions the accuracy of those accounts.

The evidence for the New Testament is overwhelming. The abundance of manuscripts removes any doubt as to the accuracy of our modern text.

II. Additional Evidence

Unlike other books, the New Testament has other sources available in addition to its original-language manuscripts by which to establish its textual reliability. Two unique sources exist for the reconstruction of the New Testament text beyond the Greek manuscripts.

1. Ancient versions.

Included in the 24,633 surviving manuscripts of the New Testament are over 15,000 copies of ancient versions. Ancient versions form a strong support for the accuracy of the text of the New Testament.

How do these ancient versions help us in reconstructing the text of the New Testament? Based on your present knowledge, consider or discuss the following questions. Indicate your opinion.

Agree or Disagree (Mark A or D)

_____1. An early version would help confirm the accurate text of Scripture if it was translated near the time of the originals.

_____2. Comparing an early version with a Greek manuscript would help substantiate the accuracy of the Greek copy, if the version was older than the Greek manuscript.

_____3. It was common for ancient books to be translated into other languages.

_____4. The New Testament was translated into many languages to assist the work of evangelism among non-Greek-speaking people.

_____5. Since the New Testament was written in Greek, Greek manuscripts are the only ones useful in determining the reliable text of the New Testament.

Ancient books were seldom translated into other languages. Due, however, to the missionary fervor inherent in Christianity, many ancient versions of the New Testament were produced to aid in the spread of Christianity among non-Greek-speaking people.

The value of those versions is seen in the fact that many versions were written around A.D. 150. That brings us very near to the time of the original. Through careful comparison, we can substantiate the accuracy of our Greek manuscripts.

Early versions are a separate line of manuscripts that help establish the historical accuracy and reliability of the New Testament text. They are well preserved and confirm the reading of the New Testament Greek manuscripts.

2. Early Church Fathers

Imagine that every New Testament manuscript, including both Greek manuscripts and ancient versions, was totally lost and destroyed. All 24,633 of them! Imagine also, that all the printed Bibles in the world were burned. Could we ever recover our Bibles?

All but 11 verses of the New Testament can be entirely reconstructed from the writings of the early church fathers without the aid of modern Bibles or handwritten manuscripts. These early church leaders and scholars who lived 150-200 years after the time of Christ, wrote sermons and articles quoting long passages of Scripture. The Scriptures were an integral part of their writings. When compared, their quotations help establish the accuracy of the New Testament text.

Based on what you've just read, how would you respond to this statement? "Maybe the church fathers did quote from the Bible a lot in their writings.

So what?"_____

_____

_____

III. Manuscript dating.

Manuscript dating is critical to the usefulness of the bibliographical test. Obviously, establishing the time gap between the original autograph and the earliest copy cannot be done without precise measures for determining manuscript dates.

Place a check beside each item in the following list of factors that you think would help fix the date of a manuscript. Refer to the key at the end of this lesson for the correct answers.

____Letter size and form
____Texture and color of the parchment
____Material used for writing
____Style of punctuation
____Color of the ink
____Ornamentation on the manuscript
____Text divisions
____Initials at the end of the manuscript

____Water stains on the manuscript
____Type of container holding the manuscript
____Size of the holes in the parchment
____Size of the scroll
____Country where the manuscript was found
____Last known manuscript owner

Conclusion

The first step in testing the reliability of the Bible is to apply the bibliographical test. It poses two questions: (1) How much time separates a copy from its original? and (2) How many manuscripts are now available for comparison and examination.

Based on the evidence of history, no other book begins to approach the Bible in manuscript authority and attestation. The wealth of bibliographical evidence attributed to the New Testament can best be seen by comparing it with textual evidence from secular sources.

The closer a copy is to the time it was originally written, the greater the accuracy the copy possesses. And the more manuscripts there are, the easier it is to confirm the original text. At least two additional resources help substantiate the text of Scripture: early versions, and the quotations of the early church fathers.

———————O———————

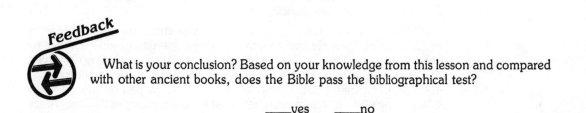

Feedback

What is your conclusion? Based on your knowledge from this lesson and compared with other ancient books, does the Bible pass the bibliographical test?

____yes   ____no

Multiple choice

Without referring to the lesson, choose the best answers to the following questions. Check the key at the end of this lesson for the correct answers.

_____1. It is important that God reveal Himself in a trustworthy document because:
  A. If God is going to be worthy of our trust we must have an accurate account of what He is like.
  B. Bible sales will drop below an acceptable level.
  C. Fewer Christians will read their Bibles.

_____2. What significance is there in determining the time gap between original composition and the closest copy?
  A. The antique value of the manuscript skyrockets.
  B. The closer in time a copy is to the original document, the more accurate it is assumed to be.
  C. The copy becomes more important than the original.

_____3. What value is there in possessing an abundance of manuscripts of an ancient book?
  A. There is less chance of the book becoming extinct.
  B. More scholars can receive original copies of an ancient book.
  C. Through comparison, it is easier to reconstruct the original text and locate discrepancies or errors.

_____4. What book in all of history is in second place in terms of the number of manuscripts and least amount of time between composition and copy?
  A. The New Testament
  B. Homer's *Iliad*
  C. Caesar's *Gallic Wars*

_____5. What use are ancient versions in substantiating the accuracy of Greek manuscripts?
  A. Early versions were translated earlier than most Greek manuscripts were copied, bringing us very close to the time of the originals.
  B. They verify that Greek was the common language at the time of Christ.
  C. They help classify first-century semitic languages.

_____6. What contribution do the early church fathers make to the use of the bibliographical test on the New Testament?
  A. The writing materials used by the church fathers is similar to the materials used for writing the New Testament.
  B. There are several thousand manuscripts of the church fathers' writings.
  C. Scripture quotations in their sermons reproduce all but 11 verses of the New Testament.

Fill-in

1. An autograph is the _____composition.

2. A manuscript is, by definition, a _____ of the original.

3. An extant manuscript is an _____manuscript.

27

4. The bibliographical test asks two questions of every ancient book:
    (1) How much time separates the _____ from the _____?

    (2) How many _____ are there?

————————————O————————————

My Response

Josh

I was lecturing in a history class in a prestigious university when the professor interrupted my talk. "The audacity," he said, "of a guest lecturer, in a history class, saying that the New Testament is reliable! That's ridiculous!"

I love it when someone says something like that, because I've always asked a question that has never yet been answered in the 605 universities I've lectured in. I replied, "Sir, as the professor of this class, as the head of this university's history department, as a scholar who has earned two Ph.Ds in history, what are the tests you use to determine the historical accuracy and reliability of any book in history?"

I thought it was a fair question.

He didn't have any answer.

I'm grateful that as true believers we don't need to be intimidated by the false skepticism of the world. God has given us more than adequate evidence on which to base our faith.

_____

(My name)

What new truth about the historical reliability of the Bible has impressed me the most?

_____

_____

_____

How will that affect my Christian walk?

_____

_____

_____

In gratitude for God's care for His Word, I will pray:

> "Father, thank You for demonstrating Your soverign control of history. You have miraculously permitted Your Word to be given to me because You love me and want to fellowship with me. Such a display of greatness demands my continued trust and dependence. Thank You for showing Yourself to be great. Amen."

For detailed documentation on the bibliographical test of the New Testament, read chapter 4 of *Evidence That Demands a Verdict,* pp. 39-52.

For a readable overview of the three tests of historiography, and how they apply to the Bible, read chapter 4, "Are the Biblical Records Reliable?" of *More Than a Carpenter,* pp. 41-59.

The evidence in this lesson can answer the question "Hasn't the New Testament been changed since it has been copied and recopied throughout history?" Read pages 4-6 in *Answers to Tough Questions.*

BIBLIOGRAPHICAL TEST
OF THE OLD TESTAMENT

A Quick Look Back

I've discovered that a trustworthy God has revealed Himself in a trustworthy way, through a reliable historical document. The bibliographical test verifies the trustworthiness of the New Testament by examining: 1) the closeness of the earliest extant copy to its original writing and 2) the number of manuscripts available for examination and comparison. I've learned that the bibliographical evidence for the new Testament surpasses that of any ten other pieces of ancient literature put together. The bibliogrphical test of the New Testament is the first step in confirming the historical accuracy and reliability of the Scripture.

——————O——————

Key Truth

The bibliographical test reveals how devoted men insured the accurate transmission of the Old Testament.

I will learn:

- how the bibliographical test confirms the accuracy of the Old Testament.
- why the Old Testament is different from other ancient books.
- what ancient scribes did to insure the accuracy of the Old Testament.

——————O——————

What Would You Say?

"You think your Old Testament is reliable? We're talking about a book, thousands of years old, that has been copied and recopied. Do you realize we're talking about a span of thousands of years? Come on, be realistic. Many different men copied the manuscripts, with many different variations. That leaves room for lots of error. To believe that those manuscripts were never intentionally altered or changed is ludicrous. The odds are too high to believe that!"

What would *you* say?

I would say _____

_____

_____

Because _____

_____

_____

——————————O——————————

Let's Lay A Foundation

It's beyond doubt that the New Testament stands up under the critical analysis of the bibliographical test. But what about the Old Testament? What manuscript authority do we have? Is the Old Testament reliable? Several factors make the use of the bibliographical test on the Old Testament unique.

I. Manuscript comparison of the Old Testament.

Do you remember the two parts of the bibliographical test? Take time to evaluate the manuscript authority of the Old Testament on the basis of the two criteria: 1) The closeness of the manuscript to the original; and 2) The number of manuscripts available for comparison.

Rank the following books according to the smallest time gap between original composition and first copy. How does the Old Testament compare?

AUTHOR	TITLE	WHEN WRITTEN	EARLIEST COPY	TIME SPAN	RANK
Homer	*Iliad*	900 B.C.	400 B.C.	500 yrs.	_____
Plato	*Tetralogies*	427-347 B.C.	A.D. 900	1200 yrs.	_____
Caesar	*Gallic Wars*	100-44 B.C.	A.D. 900	1000 yrs.	_____
Pliny the Younger	*History*	A.D. 850	A.D. 61-113	750 yrs.	_____
	Old Testament	400 B.C. (Malachi)	A.D. 1008	1400 yrs.	_____

It's obvious that the Old Testament is no better off in manuscript authority than most secular books. Does that mean the Old Testament is unreliable?

Until the discovery of the Dead Sea Scrolls in 1948, the oldest complete Hebrew manuscript was dated a full thousand years after Christ, approximately A.D. 1008. Even with the Dead Sea Scrolls, we must readily recognize we don't have the same number of extant manuscripts for the Old Testament as we have for the New. When we come to the Old Testament, however, (and this is true of no other book), we discover that the lack of early manuscripts in no way detracts from the accuracy and authority of the Old Testament.

I can imagine someone saying: "Now, just a minute, McDowell. We spent an entire lesson studying about the abundance of manuscripts of the New Testament, the closeness in time, what gives authority to a manuscript and how important that is, and now you're trying to say the lack of early manuscripts in no way takes away from the reliability of the Old Testament?"

That's right! And what I'm saying will appear more reasonable when you consider the facts.

II. Standards of the Old Testament manuscript transmission.

When we take into account the standards and procedures set by the Jews in transcribing the Scriptures we can understand the statement that the lack of early manuscripts in no way affects the reliability of the Old Testament.

1. Honor for the Scriptures.

The Jews have a deep reverence for Scripture. That reverence has been cultivated for centuries through their history. At the close of the Jewish exile, a remnant of God's people returned to Palestine under the leadership of Nehemiah and Ezra. They had for several years been without instruction from God's Word. True worship of Yahweh had been lost.

Glance over Nehemiah 8 and respond to the following. How does the response of this newly returned people exhibit their love for God's Word?

What did the people ask Ezra to do for them?

Nehemiah 8:1 – _____

How long did the people stay, listening to Ezra?

Nehemiah 8:3 – _____

How did the people respond to Ezra's ministry of the Word?

Nehemiah 8:5-6 – _____

Ezra may have been one of the first to organize team teaching. How did they make certain the people understood?

Nehemiah 8:7-8 – _____

Another example of Israel's reverence for the Scriptures occurred under King Josiah, shortly before Judah was deported into exile. Investigate 2 Chronicles 34 and reply to the following.

In repairing God's house, what did they discover?

Vs. 14 – _____

What was King Josiah's response to the contents of this book?

Vss. 18-21 – _____

What importance did Josiah place on this book in the national life of Israel?

Vss. 30-33 – _____

2. Transcription of the Scriptures.

It's not surprising that a nation who esteemed its Scripture so highly would produce a class of men solely devoted to the care and copying of the Scriptures. One such man was Ezra.

What was Ezra's occupation?

Ezra 7:6 – _____

What was Ezra's motivation?

Ezra 7:10 – _____

Among the Jews were a professional class of men called scribes. Scribes were professional copyists, specially trained in the knowledge and transcription of the Scriptures. These scribes would laboriously copy and recopy each manuscript, insuring its survival for later generations. Ezra is spoken of as a skilled scribe, purposing to study, apply, and teach God's law. Ezra exemplifies the devoted reverence of the scribes to God's law.

Among the scribes, two groups were significant in the preservation of Scripture. One was the Talmudic scribes. From about A.D. 100 to A.D. 400 the Talmudic scribes spent time cataloging Hebrew civil and ceremonial law, as well as transcribing Scripture. The second group was the Massoretic scribes. From about A.D. 500 to A.D. 900 the Massoretic scribes standardized the Hebrew text, adding vowel points to insure proper pronunciation.

(1) The copyists' rules.

The Talmudic and Massoretic scribes followed strict disciplines in copying the Scriptures. They pledged their lives to the meticulous care of God's Word. They devised a complicated system of safeguards to eliminate error.

Here is a list of disciplines the scribes followed in copying the Scriptures. Place a check beside the ones you think would aid in accurately copying the Word of God.

____The scroll must be prepared by a Jew from the skin of a clean animal.

____A special recipe of black ink must be used.

____Between each letter must be a space the size of a thread.

____The fifth book of Moses must terminate exactly at the end of a line.

____The scribe must refuse to acknowledge the presence of a king when writing God's name.

____The scribe must count each consonant, and indicate the center consonant.

____If more than three mistakes occur, the scribe must destroy the manuscript.

____The manuscript must contain a certain number of columns, equal throughout the entire book.

____The scribe must copy letter by letter, not word for word, trusting nothing to memory.

____Between each book the scribe must leave three lines.

____The scribe must sit in full Jewish dress.

____The scribe must count the number of times each letter of the alphabet occurs in each book.

____The scribe must count each word, and indicate the center word.

____All of the above.

By following that system of a discipline and calculation, the scribes could tell if a single letter, consonant or word was lost or added. They would know if one word was missing by comparing the totals with the master total. If there was a discrepancy, they knew a mistake existed.

(2) The copyists' importance.

The key to the application of the bibliographical test to the Old Testament is in the copyists' standards of transcription. When they produced a master copy, they were so certain it was an exact duplicate, they gave the new copy equal authority as the old copy. Since each new manuscript was an exact duplicate of the last, the new manuscript was as authentic as the old. With the New Testament, we generally give greater authority to the old manuscript. But not here. With Old Testament manuscripts, age was a distinct disadvantage. Ancient manuscripts age and decay. The lettering becomes indistinct and obscure.

The old manuscripts helped school boys learn to read. Eventually, they were destroyed. That is the reason we do not have many Old Testament manuscripts – the Jews buried them.

Is it any wonder, then, that the Biblical manuscripts have survived with such continuity and accuracy? What at first appears as useless trivia, in effect manifests the scribes' deep motivation to preserve and insure God's Word. the Talmudic and Massoretic scribes were anxious that not one jot, tittle or the smallest part of a letter of the law pass away or be lost. The very absence of ancient manuscripts, when the rules of the copyists are considered, confirms the reliability of the Old Testament.

An example of the copyists' accuracy is the evidence of the Dead Sea Scrolls, containing Old Testament manuscripts a thousand years older than previously possessed. Suddenly, a thousand years of copyists' work was bridged, giving opportunity to evaluate the accuracy of the copyists.

One of the Dead Sea Scrolls is a complete text of Isaiah. When compared, only 17 letters of the 166 words in Isaiah 53 are in question. Fourteen of those letters are simply a matter of style and spelling. The remaining three letters spell the word "light." Thus in one chapter of 166 words only one word of three letters is in question after a thousand years of transmission. And the word does not greatly affect the meaning of the passage!

In the history of documents, such a phenomenon is a miracle. It certainly confirms not only the reliability of our Old Testament text but also God's great providence. It also confirms the respect of the Jews for their Scriptures.

Conclusion

The scribes preserved not the oldest Old Testament manuscript, but the latest! Why? Because of the Jews' reverence for the Scripture. Considering the disciplines followed by the scribes in copying the Scriptures, an old manuscript had no advantage over a new manuscript. Each was an exact copy of the other. Age would have no advantage because misunderstandings could occur from worn, indistinct lettering. The accuracy and reliability of Old Testament manuscripts are reinforced by the discovery of the Dead Sea Scrolls, closing a thousand-year gap and showing no appreciable differences when compared.

————————O————————

Feedback

1. How does the Old Testament compare with other works of antiquity, considering the time gap between original composition and first copy, and the number of manuscripts?

   _____

   _____

   _____

2. What key factor changes the application of the bibliographical test to the Old Testament?

_____

_____

_____

3. Name two scribal traditions that demonstrate the carefulness with which the Scriptures were copied.

   (1) _____

   (2) _____

4. What disciplines followed by the scribes in copying the Scriptures impressed you the most? Why?

_____

_____

_____

5. How would you reply to this statement: "The historical reliability of the Old Testament is questionable because very few manuscripts exist, and there is a wide gap between the originals and the copies."?

_____

_____

_____

————————O————————

My Response

Josh

I teach the material in this lesson in our "6 Hours" conference. We developed a video illustration of a scribe copying the Scriptures and invited an Orthodox Rabbi to be our scribe. We used a four-hundred-year-old manuscript of Esther as the authentic scroll with a similated leather scroll as the copy. Everything was ready. Laboriously, the Rabbi demonstrated the scribal technique on video. When in his copying, he came to the name of God, he did a curious thing. He refused to write out the full name of God! He would only write the first two letters, enough for us to show on video how a scribe would begin to write the name of God.

I was puzzled. Why wouldn't he write God's name? When asked, he replied, "This is not an authentic scroll that will be handled according to Talmudic law. God's name is too sacred to be written on something that will be destroyed and not reverently used in the synagogue."

That taught me a lesson. We returned the scroll of Esther to the museum. But, we kept the simulated scroll as a reminder of the devoted men through the centuries who so carefully preserved God's Word. I'm indebted to them!

_____

(My name)

How has this lesson increased my appreciation for God's Word?

_____

_____

_____

How will my approach to the Scriptures be different as a result of this study?

_____

_____

_____

In gratitude for God's care over His Word, I will pray:

> *"Thank You, Father, for the dedicated men who reverenced Your Word so much that they devoted their lives to its care. Because of them, I hold Your Word in my hands today. I am humbled and motivated to imitate their commitment to the care of Your truth. Amen."*

————————O————————

For Further Reference

A detailed presentation of evidence for the reliability of the Old Testament is found in *Evidence That Demands a Verdict*, pp. 52-60.

For a succinct analysis of the Dead Sea Scrolls discovery read, "How Do the Dead Sea Scrolls Relate to Biblical Criticism?" pp. 25-27, in *Answers to Tough Questions*.

INTERNAL EVIDENCE TEST

A Quick Look Back

I've discovered how the bibliographical test confirms the accuracy with which our Bible was transmitted through the centuries. Because of the devoted care of men who love God's Word, I can read my Bible with confidence, knowing it contains a reliable record of the apostles' and prophets' writings.

———————O———————

Key Truth

The internal evidence test demonstrates that the content of the Bible is credible and reliable.

I will learn:

- what makes a document historically accurate.
- the motivation apparent discrepancies in the Bible provide for intense Bible study.
- the principles to follow in evaluating supposed Bible inconsistencies.

———————O———————

What Would You Say?

"Do you really believe that the Bible can be trusted? Come on! Look at all those discrepancies; the Bible is loaded with hundreds of contradictions. There's no way that I can base what I believe on a book that is so full of errors."

What would *you* say?

I would say _____

_____

_____

Because _____

_____

_____

———————————O———————————

Let's Lay A Foundation

The internal evidence test evaluates the content of a document on its own merits, seeking out factual inaccuracies or obvious contradictions. It determines if what is said is believable. In other words, this test evaluates the internal claims of a document to judge its credibility. Two major principles guide the application of this test.

I. PRINCIPLE 1: An author is innocent until proven guilty of a discrepancy.

In the event of an apparent factual inaccuracy, the benefit of the doubt must be given to the document under examination. The reader must not form a hasty judgment. And in the case of inadequate evidence, a favorable decision goes to the document. One must honestly listen to the claims under examination without assuming error in advance. In the case of obvious contradictions, the author disqualifies himself.

When confronting apparent discrepancies in the Bible, keep in mind these three reminders:

Reminder 1 – The Bible's claim to inerrancy applies only to the original autographs, not the copies.

Reminder 2 – The list of apparent contradictions is getting shorter, not longer, as modern scholarship is applied to the Scriptures.

Reminder 3 – Time is on your side in resolving textual difficulties.

Over the past 25 years, the list of apparent biblical discrepancies has been cut to one-fourth. Discrepancies have been slowly reduced year by year through further insight into word meanings, manuscript evidence, archeology and textual study.

Paul's Conversion – An Apparent Discrepancy

Using the King James Version, compare these passages about Paul's conversion. Note the similarities and then the differences.

Acts 9:7   Acts 22:9

SIMILARITIES	
"And the _____ which _____ with him..."	"And _____ that _____ with me..."
"...stood _____"	"...saw indeed the
	light and _____"

DIFFERENCES	
"...hearing a _____	"...they heard _____
but _____."	of him that spake to me"

40

Acts 9:7 states they *did* hear a voice, but they saw no one speaking. Acts 22:9 clearly states that they *did not* hear the voice of the one speaking to Paul. Is this a clear-cut discrepancy? How can we resolve it?

Now, compare those same verses in the New American Standard Bible. How do the disputed phrases read?

"And the men who traveled with him stood speechless, _____

_____, but_____" (Acts 9:7).

"And those who were with me beheld the light, to be sure, but did not

_____ the _____ of the One who was _____ to me" (Acts 22:9).

Based on this comparison, how would you harmonize these accounts?

_____

_____

_____

The key is in the construction and translation of the verbs. The verb "to hear" is not the same in both accounts. In Acts 22:9 the verb is used in conjunction with an accusative noun. Research shows this means, "did not *comprehend* the voice." In Acts 9 the verb is used with the genitive, meaning they simply heard a sound. The two accounts combine to show that Paul's companions heard a voice but they didn't understand it. Acts 22:9 does not deny that they heard a voice, but simply adds that they did not understand what they heard. The New American Standard version takes advantage of recent advances in language meanings and textual studies.

A possible explanation for why Paul's companions did not understand the voice is suggested by a third account of Paul's conversion in Acts 26:14:

The voice spoke in a language, possibly foreign to Paul's companions, Jewish Aramaic.

II. PRINCIPLE 2: The nearness of an author to the events recorded affects his credibility.

The closeness of an author, both geographically and chronologically to the events he records, is extremely important. If a writer records hearsay, his credibility is suspect. If he records personal experience, or first-hand reports, his credibility is enhanced.

How does this affect the New Testament?

1. The New Testament writers were eye witnesses or recorded eyewitness accounts.

   The New Testament was written by men who either personally knew Jesus or recorded personal accounts. That is stated in Scriptures.

   Look up each Scripture passage and do the following:

   (1) Locate each phrase that indicates eyewitness testimony.

   (2) Write out that phrase beside the Scripture reference.

   (3) Record any insights you may have.

41

SCRIPTURE	EYEWITNESS TESTIMONY	INSIGHTS
Act 1:3	1. To these He _____ 2. By many _____ 3. _____ over a period of 40 days 4. And _____ the kingdom of God	
1 John 1:1-3	1. What we _____ 2. What we have _____ with_____ 3. What we _____ and our _____ 4. And _____ and bear witness 5. Which was with the Father and_____ 6. What _____ we proclaim to you	
2 Peter 1:16-18	1. We did not follow _____ 2. But we were _____ 3. And we _____ from heaven 4. When we _____ on the holy mountain	
John 20:30	1. Many other _____ therefore Jesus _____ 2. In the _____ of the _____	

The historian Luke typifies a Scripture writer who was not himself an eyewitness. Luke recorded eyewitness accounts in the same manner as a modern day reporter. He gives us an insight into his method.

"Inasmuch as many have undertaken to _____ of the things _____, just as those who from the beginning were _____ and servants of the word have _____, it seemed fitting for me as well, having _____ from the beginning, to _____ in _____, most excellent Theophilus" (Luke 1:1-3).

The closeness of a writer to the events he records effectively certifies the accuracy of his reports. Without firsthand knowledge, he is largely unreliable.

But what of the eyewitness who consciously or unconsciously tells falsehoods? Is there a further test to determine even an eyewitness's truthfulness?

2. The New Testament writers appealed to the knowledge of their hearers and readers.

The apostles based their message on the knowledge their hearers had concerning Christ. Two facts support this.

(1) Their opponents knew that what was said was true.

The facts on which the Christian faith is based (the life, death and resurrection of Christ) occurred over a long period of time and were observed by plenty of witnesses. Many think that only a handful of people were acquainted with the facts of Jesus' life. But the disciples bore witness to events that were common knowledge. Not only did the disciples know the facts, but their enemies did as well! It was common for early Christians to challenge their most hostile opponents with, "You saw these things also."

Did Peter take time to convince his audience of the facts surrounding Jesus' life?

"Men of Israel, listen to these words: Jesus the Nazarene, a man

_____ with miracles and wonders and signs which

God performed through Him _____, just as _____"
(Acts 2:22).

Later, in the same sermon, Peter make this statement:

"This Jesus God raised up again, to which _____"
(Acts 2:32).

Paul followed a similar strategy.

"And while Paul was saying this in his defense, Festus said in a loud voice, 'Paul, you are out of your mind! Your great learning is driving you mad.'

"But Paul said, 'I am not out of my mind, most excellent Festus,

but I _____.

For the King _____,

and I _____

_____, since I am persuaded that _____

_____; for _____

_____"(Acts 26:24-26).

Early preachers of Christianity were confident their hearers knew that what was being said was true. Both sides knew the facts. The discussion was not about the facts, but about the conclusive evidence those facts presented about Christ's identity.

(2) Their opponents could refute what was said if it were false.

   If you base your argument on facts your enemy knows, you had better
be right, or it will be used against you. If the apostles made false claims,
Christ's opponents could refute them. If early Christians had dared to depart
from the truth, those who knew better would have immediately corrected
it. The fact that the enemies of Christ could not do so is eloquent testimony
to the truthfulness and accuracy of the disciples' eyewitness reports.

Conclusion

   The internal evidence test seeks to determine the credibility of what is actually recorded. In evaluating historical documents, it operates on two principles. First, an author
is innocent until proven guilty of a discrepancy, and second, the nearness of an author
to the events recorded affects his credibility.

   Alleged discrepancies of the Bible are often resolved by intense study. New under-
standings of difficult passages comes from recent linguistic and archeological evidence.
Also, the New Testament writers were best qualified to record the events of Christ's
life, because they were either eyewitnesses or recorded eyewitness accounts. Further-
more, the early Christians attested to the truthfulness of their message by appealing
to the knowledge of their hearers, confident that they spoke nothing false.

————————O————————

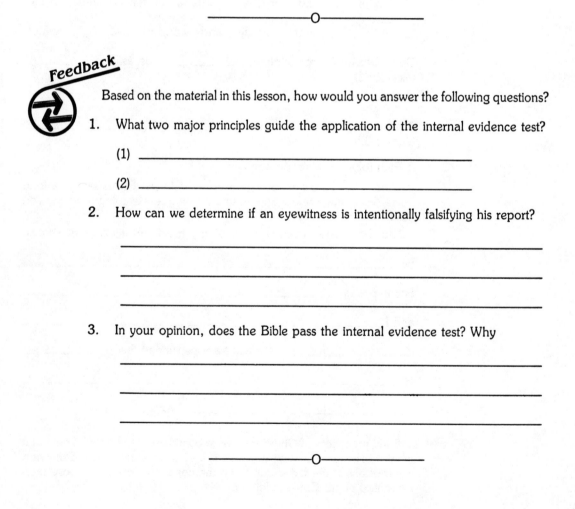

Feedback

Based on the material in this lesson, how would you answer the following questions?

1. What two major principles guide the application of the internal evidence test?

    (1) _____

    (2) _____

2. How can we determine if an eyewitness is intentionally falsifying his report?

    _____

    _____

    _____

3. In your opinion, does the Bible pass the internal evidence test? Why

    _____

    _____

    _____

————————O————————

My Response

I've often been asked, "Mr. McDowell, how do you know that the Bible is true? What about all the discrepancies in the Bible?" I admit that I don't have all the answers and there are some puzzling questions I have yet to resolve. But the overwhelming evidence is for the accuracy and reliability of the Bible. The weight of the evidence is on the side of the Bible's being true. The remaining alleged contradictions I leave to God, in faith, believing that new facts and truths will unravel the puzzle. But a list of apparent contradictions doesn't undermine my faith. It motivates me to study harder. History shows that the more we study and understand, the shorter the list grows.

_____

(My name)

What new truth have I learned about God's Word in this lesson?

_____

_____

_____

How will that affect my relationship with Christ?

_____

_____

_____

What doubts have I had about the reliability of God's Word that have been resolved by this lesson?

_____

_____

_____

In response to God's goodness in providing us with a trustworthy revelation, I will pray:

"Father, I'm grateful for the truthfulness of Your Word. Since it is true in areas it can be tested, by faith I acknowledge its authority over every area of my life, even in areas where it can't be tested. Thank You for fulfilling Your Word in my life. Amen."

For Further Reference

Two articles in *Answers to Tough Questions* particularly relate to this lesson: "How can anyone believe the New Testament account of the life of Jesus, seeing that it was written long after His death?", pages 7-8; and "How can you believe a Bible that is full of contradictions?", pages 15-17.

For a detailed review of the internal evidence test read, *Evidence That Demands a Verdict*, pp. 61-63.

To understand how crucial the three tests of historical research are to the basis of our Christian faith, especially the internal evidence test, read observation 9 in *The Resurrection Factor*, pp. 24-35.

EXTERNAL EVIDENCE TEST

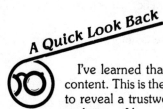

I've learned that the internal evidence test confirms the consistency of the Bible's content. This is the second major step in determining the reliability of a book that claims to reveal a trustworthy God. By following the principles for evaluating alleged contradictions, I have gained a greater confidence in the credibility and reliability of the Bible.

―――――――――○―――――――――

Key Truth

The external evidence test uses outside sources to confirm the inner testimony of Scripture.

I will learn:

- how archeology helps prove the trustworthiness of the Bible.
- how the early church fathers help us know the Bible is true.
- how Luke is considered a reliable historian.

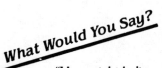

"You might believe what the Bible says just because it is in print. But I'm not that gullible. Just because somebody writes something doesn't make it true. You might think that the people who wrote the Bible are to be believed, but how do we know they wrote it? Besides, there is a lot of archaeological evidence that disproves the Bible."

What would *you* say?

I would say _____

_____

_____

Because _____

_____

_____

―――――――――○―――――――――

A Quick Look Back

What Would You Say?

LESSON 5

Proving the reliability of the Bible verifies God's trustworthiness. If the Bible is trustworthy, that's one more reason why God can be trusted. This lesson discusses the third and final test for determining the historical reliability of the Bible – the external evidence test.

The issue in this test is whether *other* historical material confirms or substantiates the testimony of the Bible. In other words, what sources are there that substantiate the Bible's accuracy, reliability and authenticity? Are there other historical documents, written during the same period of time, that confirm the Bible's inner testimony? Conformity and agreement with other known historical or scientific facts is a decisive factor in the external evidence test.

Two outside sources confirm the inner testimony of the Bible – the writings of the early church fathers, and archaeology.

I. Confirmation by Extra-Biblical Authors

Writers from the early centuries of Christianity give us good insight into the conditions surrounding the writing of the New Testament. These writers confirm historical detail, authorship and contents of several New Testament books.

1. Polycarp confirms the Apostles' reports.

Polycarp, martyred at age 86 in A.D. 156, was Bishop of Smyrna and a disciple of the apostle John. Polycarp knew John personally and was likely in his late twenties when the apostle died in about A.D. 98. Polycarp certainly had plenty of contacts with the apostles and is qualified to confirm the accuracy of their reports. One of Polycarp's students, Irenaus, preserves his testimony of the certainty of the gospel records. Irenaus, then, was just two generations away from the apostles, the companions of Christ.

THE POLYCARP BRIDGE

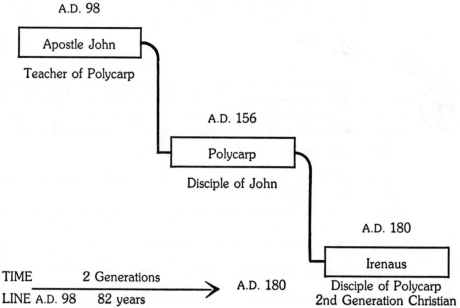

A.D. 98

Apostle John

Teacher of Polycarp

A.D. 156

Polycarp

Disciple of John

A.D. 180

Irenaus

TIME 2 Generations → A.D. 180
LINE A.D. 98 82 years

Disciple of Polycarp
2nd Generation Christian

Irenaus records a direct outside testimony (Polycarp) to the accuracy of the apostles' reports. To better understand the significance of this external evidence, answer the following multiple choice questions by circling the most logical answer.

_____1. To confirm the accuracy of the apostles' writings by external evidence, whose documented testimony would be more valid?

    A. The apostle John's distant cousin who lived 300 years after John died.

    B. Polycarp, a companion of the apostles, as recorded by his disciple, Irenaus.

    C. A brilliant German historian conjecturing on the apostles' method of recording gospel accounts.

_____2. What valuable information would Irenaus have that others would not have?

    A. Polycarp was a companion of John.

    B. Polycarp died a martyr's death.

    C. Direct quotations from conversations Polycarp had with the apostle John.

_____3. How would you rate the value of Irenaus's recording testimony of the apostles' reports from the mouth of an eyewitness (Polycarp).

    A. Irrelevant testimony.

    B. Weak testimony.

    C. Confirming testimony.

2. Polycarp confirms the testimony of the heretics.

These are Polycarp's words:

"So firm is the ground upon which these Gospels rest, that the very heretics themselves bear witness to them, and, starting from these, each one of them endeavors to establish his own particular doctrine."

Irenaus quoting Polycarp in
Against Heresies III

The accuracy of the gospel accounts of Christ's life and ministry were so established that the heretics could not even refute them. The enemies of Christianity had to start with the accepted, historical facts and distort the meaning to arrive at their false conclusions.

Again, answer the following multiple choice questions by circling the most logical answer.

_____1. The heretics didn't refute the apostles' accounts of Christ because:

    A. The events were too insignificant to comment about.

    B. No one accepted the apostles' recorded accounts as reliable.

    C. They couldn't refute the historical accuracy of the accounts, only the interpretation of them.

_____2. External evidence confirms the accuracy of recorded accounts when:

    A. All your friends agree the documented accounts are accurate.

    B. Your enemies agree the accounts cannot be refuted.

    C. Half of the people agree the documented accounts are accurate and half dispute it.

Polycarp's testimony, preserved by Irenaus, confirms the reliability of the biblical accounts. Others include Papias, Bishop of Hieropolis, A.D. 130; Ignatius, Bishop of Antioch, A.D. 110; and many others.

II. Confirmation through archaeology.

Another significant factor in the external evidence test is archaeology. Archaeology confirms many of the historical and cultural elements of the biblical narrative. While archaeology does not prove that the Bible is true, it can confirm the historical accuracy of the setting in which the Bible was written. It serves as an external check on the historical accuracy and reliability of the biblical narrative.

1. Kingdom of Ebla.

A significant archaeological find that relates to the external confirmation of the internal witness of the Bible is the ancient Kingdom of Ebla. Much yet remains to be finalized from that remarkable discovery, but there are several important Bible related facts to consider.

Two archaeologists from the University of Rome, unearthed in Syria one of the greatest third millenium B.C. archives ever discovered. Since 1974, archaeologists have uncovered more thant 17,000 tablets, yielding a rare glimpse into an unknown kingdom. The tablets contain census figures, geographical names, legislative codes, religious essays, bureaucratic rostrums, dictionaries and other literary aids. The contents of these tablets struck the scholarly world like a thunderbolt.

How would you use the evidence discovered at the kingdom of Ebla dig in the external evidence test of the Bible? To answer each of the following criticisms, choose the conclusion you think is most appropriate based on evidence given.

Criticism 1: Moses could not have written the Pentateuch, because writing did not exist in Moses' day. Moses lived 3,500 years ago, about 1400 B.C., and civilization was too primitive for the knowledge of writing to exist.

Ebla Find: Kingdom of Ebla tablets show that writing existed as early as 2400 B.C., 4,500 years ago. Laws, customs, events, directories and essays were recorded in writing. Even graffiti existed in Ebla!

Conclusion:

____A. This was a freak situation and no other group at that time period had writing skills except the Ebla civilization.

____B. This is evidence that writing skills existed in Moses' day and he could have written the Pentateuch.

____C. Only royal proceedings were put in writing. Common people did not possess writing skills.

Criticism 2: The various uses of the names for God in the Pentateuch (Jehovah, El Shaddai, Elohim, etc.) indicate more than one author. The Pentateuch is a compilation of the sentiments of several authors, each giving a different name to God. No early writer would use more than one name for God in the same narrative.

Ebla Find: At the kingdom of Ebla site, a Canaanite text was discovered which was dated at the same time Moses and the Patriarchs lived. This text used five different names for God in a single narrative.

Conclusion:

____A. It would not be uncommon for Moses to use more than one name for God in writing the Pentateuch, since describing God's greatness requires various names.

____B. The Eblite writer was confused and couldn't decide what name to use for his god.

____C. The Ebla tablet is an exception. Other religious writings would still only use one name for God at a time.

Criticism 3: The priestly and moral codes recorded in the Pentateuch are far too advanced to have been written by Moses. The Israelite nation was too primitive in Moses' lifetime to have devised such intricate regulations. It was not until a thousand years *after* Moses that such detailed legislation was recorded.

Ebla Find: Law codes were discovered in the Ebla tablets containing elaborate and detailed judicial proceedings and case law. These tablets were dated a thousand years *before* Moses.

Conclusion:

_____A.   The writers of these tablets just fabricated these cases such as we do today in science fiction.

_____B.   This is confirmation that the civilization prior to and around the time of Moses was cultured and that the Israelite nation was not primitive.

_____C.   The tablets were dated wrong.

2. The Accuracy of Luke

For many years Bible critics assumed that the Book of Acts was riddled with error. They said Luke's historical references were unsubstantiated by outside sources. However, as a result of investigation by archaeologist Sir William Ramsay, scholarly opinion has changed regarding Luke's skill as an historian.

Many critics doubted the accuracy of Luke's choices of titles for various Roman and pagan officials.

(1) What title did Luke ascribe to the Philippian rulers?

Acts 16:20,22 – _____

Luke used the title "praetor" meaning a chief magistrate. For years scholars insisted that Luke was incorrect in calling such rulers "praetors." According to scholars two "duumuirs" would have ruled the town. However, recent findings have shown that the Philippian rulers preferred the more dignified title "praetor" over "duumuir."

(2) What title did Luke use to apply to Gallio?

Acts 18:12 – _____

Specialists in Roman history for years maintained that Gallio could not have been a proconsul. In their view there was no room in Gallio's life for such an important post as proconsul. Clearly, Luke was wrong.

But Luke's accuracy was reinforced by an inscription discovered in Delphi that refers to Gallio as the proconsul of Achaia. The Delphi inscription, dated A.D. 52, gives us a fixed date for the ministry of the apostle Paul in Corinth. We know that Gallio's proconsulship lasted only one year, and that year overlapped Paul's work in Corinth.

(3) What expression does Luke use to describe Publius, a prominent man in Malta who befriended the Apostle Paul?

Acts 28:7 – _____

Many critics considered Luke's reference to Publius as no more than descriptive of his social status. Luke's reputation as a meticulous historian was vindicated by the unearthing of an inscription which gave Publius the title of "first man." That is further evidence of Luke's ability as a historian.

There can be no doubt that archaeology has confirmed the Bible as a reliable book of history. Each turn of the archaeologist's spade has confirmed the view that the Bible is a reliable source of history.

Conclusion

The external evidence test confirms the accuracy and reliability of the Bible from outside sources. The early church fathers confirm the accuracy of the apostles' reports and the certainty with which the gospel record was accepted as historically true. Even their enemies could not refute them! Archaeology also confirms the accuracy of biblical reports. Discoveries in the kingdom of Ebla confirm the Mosaic narrative and Luke has been vindicated in his reporting of historical details.

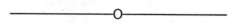

Feedback

True or False

See the key at the end of the lesson for correct answers.

_____1. The Bible has two outside confirmations of its inner accuracy: extrabiblical authors and archaeology.

_____2. Polycarp's testimony recorded by Irenaus is irrelevant because Polycarp wasn't a historian.

_____3. While archaeology does not prove the Bible true, it can confirm the historical accuracy of the setting in which the Bible was written.

_____4. The kingdom of Ebla discovery confirms many of the historical facts of the internal message of the Bible.

_____5. Luke, the writer of Acts, was an unskilled historian because he didn't even know the correct titles of pagan and Roman officials.

My Response

Josh

As a skeptic, I set out to refute Christianity. A number of historical facts, however, had a tremendous impact upon me. One was that no one refuted the miraculous events the apostles ascribed to Christ. They changed the meaning, but not the facts. I had an intellectual battle. I attempted to rule out miracles and the Resurrection. Yet, the more I investigated history the more intellectually ridiculous my conclusions became. If I was to be intellectually honest, I had to face facts! Christ was who He said He was! After an intense struggle, I submitted my life to Christ. The evidence was not the issue, it was my will. I've seen that repeated in many lives – the issue is not intellectual, but moral. Will I submit my life to Christ's control?

_____

(My name)

How has the testimony of external sources deepened my trust in God's Word?

_____

_____

List any doubts about the historic accuracy of the Bible that have been resolved as a result of this lesson.

_____

_____

_____

In response to God providing a trustworthy revelation of Himself, I will pray:

"Lord Jesus, thank You for Your Word that has proven reliable and trustworthy. The accuracy of the Bible witnesses to Your trustworthiness. Right now I reaffirm my trust in You. Thank You for being Lord of my life. Amen."

————————————————O————————————————

For Further Reference

For more detailed evidence on the external confirmation of Scripture, read *Evidence That Demands a Verdict*, pp. 63-74.

For a helpful analysis of the contribution of archaeology to the trustworthiness of Scripture, read *More Evidence That Demands a Verdict*, pp. 17-22.

Does archaeology prove the Bible? For an answer read, *Answers to Tough Questions*, pp. 23-24.

Section 2

GOD CAN BE TRUSTED: QUALIFICATIONS FOR TRUSTWORTHINESS

GOD IS THE FINAL AUTHORITY

A Quick Look Back

I now know that the most important step in investigating God's trustworthiness is demonstrating that the Bible is trustworthy. It's a trustworthy record of God's work in history. A trustworthy God has revealed Himself in a trustworthy way. I've discovered that the Bible meets the criteria of trustworthiness, being reliable according to the standard tests applied to any book of history: the bibliographical, internal and external evidence tests. I study this historically reliable book, the Bible, to discover the kind of God described in its pages. I will identify the qualities of God's character that make Him worthy of my trust.

———————O———————

Key Truth

God can be trusted because He is the final authority, having complete and exclusive rights to everything.

I will learn:

- that God has exclusive rights.
- that Christ has been given full authority.
- what is the basis on which I receive my rights.

———————O———————

What Would You Say?

"I've always said religious promises were designed to spark hope in the human heart. They are not promises to be taken literally. Rather, let them be ideals you work toward; let them ignite that inner hope to drive you toward your dreams. You'll be disappointed unless you do all in your own ability to fulfill each promise you make to yourself."

What would *you* say?

I would say _____

_____

_____

Because _____

_____

_____

Let's Lay A Foundation

What qualifications does God possess that make Him worthy of our trust? In this lesson we will discuss the first qualification of trustworthiness – authority.

Suppose you walked into your local bank to apply for a loan and met the bank janitor at the door. "You need money?" he asks. "Trust me, I'll get it for you. I work here."

It's unlikely that I would trust a bank janitor to process my loan request, even if he did say, "Trust me, I work here." I would doubt his word because I am convinced that a bank janitor does not have sufficient authority to grant loan requests. Before I trust someone I must be convinced he is sufficiently authorized to carry out his claim. I wouldn't trust the janitor for a loan unless I knew that the janitor was really the bank president doing double duty!

If a person is to be trusted he must have the authority to fulfill what he's trusted for.

Authority over any matter is often linked to ownership rights. If I own something, it's mine. I have the right or authority to use what I own in the manner I think best.

How is that concept applied to our trust relationship with God? Can I be certain God is worthy of my complete trust?

I. God has complete ownership rights.

Scripture declares that God has authority over all things because He owns all things. Everything belongs to God. That is the foundation of my trust in God. I am wise to trust God fully if He alone has rights to everything.

1. God has created all things.

God possesses rights to everything by right of creation. He made it! Therefore, it belongs to God. According to Genesis 1:1 all things were created by God. He established His right of possession by right of creation.

King David acknowledged that God owns the world because He made it.

"For the Lord is a great God, And a great King above all gods, in

_____ are the _____;

the peaks of the mountains are _____.

The sea _____, for it was _____;

and _____." (Psalm 95:3-5).

Again, David truly understood that the world belongs to God.

"The _____ is the Lord's, and _____

_____, the _____, and those _____

_____" (Psalm 24:1).

58

Scripture makes clear that the earth and everything in it belongs to God.

2. God has given life to all things.

God not only has ownership rights over all His creation, but He also is the very source of life.

According to Genesis 2:7, how did man become a living soul?

_____

_____

_____

Adam received the gift of life from God. He did not become a living, breathing, functioning person until God personally breathed life into his human form.

Is there any parallel between Adam receiving life as a gift from God and our having existence? What new awareness should this realization create in us?

Isaiah 42: 5 – _____

_____

_____

What happens at death that demonstrates that God is the author of life?

Ecclesiastes 12:7 – _____

_____

_____

Since God is the source of life, to whom, then, do we belong?

"For if we live, we live _____, or if we die,

we die _____; therefore

whether we live or die, we _____.

For to this end Christ died and lived again, that _____

_____" (Romans 14:8,9).

II. All rights have been given to His Son.

1. The Son receives authority from the Father.

How much authority has been given to Christ?

(1) God has placed Him in the position of authority.

And God has "seated Him at His right hand in the heavenly places,

far above _____ and _____

and _____, and every _____

that is _____, not only in _____,

but also in _____

_____" (Ephesians 1:20-21).

(2) God has given Him the exercise of authority.

"For in Him all the fullness of Deity dwells in bodily form, and in Him

you have been made complete, and He is_____

over _____

_____" (Colossians 2:9-10).

(3) God has given Him the recognition of authority.

"Therefore also God _____, and bestowed on Him the

_____,

that at the name of Jesus _____

of those...in heaven...on earth,...and that _____

_____ that Jesus Christ is Lord, to the glory of God the
Father" (Philippians 2:9-11).

All God's rights have been given to the Son. Therefore, He can be trusted
too!

2. We receive our rights through the Son.

God owns all rights to everything, and has chosen to give those rights to
His Son. As redeemed children, what rights do we regain through Christ?

"For you have not received a spirit of slavery leading to fear again, but

you have received a _____

_____ by which we cry out,

'_____!' The Spirit Himself bears witness with our

spirit that we are_____

_____" (Romans 8:15-16).

What does this relationship give us the right to be?

"And if children,_____ also, _____ of God and

_____ with Christ" (Romans 8:17).

"But as many as received Him, to them_____

_____ to become _____

_____, even to those who believe in His name" (John 1:12).

We regain in Christ what was lost through Satan. That's the meaning of
salvation – restoring all that is rightfully ours.

All the rights that God owns Christ shares with us. When we become children of God we become heirs to His kingdom and co-owners of all that God has.

Conclusion

God has full authority and rights over every aspect of life, qualifying Him to be trusted. Trust is initially based on the authority a person possesses, the rightful authorization to carry out his word. Since God has complete and exclusive rights to everything, I can consider all His claims as authoritative. God can be trusted on the basis of His final authority.

———————O———————

Feedback

Fill-in

Without referring to the material you've just covered, fill in the blank spaces below. To check your answers, refer to the key at the end of this lesson.

1. If a person is to be trusted he must have_____ to fulfill what he's trusted for.

2. Before I trust someone, I must be convinced he is sufficiently author-

    ized to _____.

3. God possesses rights to everything by right of_____

    _____ .

4. All God's rights have been given to _____.

    Therefore, _____!

5. When we become _____ of God we become _____ to His

    kingdom and _____ of all that God has.

Matching:

Connect each Scripture with the truth it expresses. See the key for answers.

1. Colossians 2:9,10   A. Everything belongs to God because He made it.

2. Isaiah 42:5   B. We are dependent on God for every breath we breathe.

3. Psalm 95:3-5   C. God, the Son possesses the authority of God, the Father.

4. Romans 8:15-17   D. Through Christ we became co-owners with God, regaining all we lost to Satan.

My Response

Josh

One evening I watched with interest as two of my children played tug-of-war with a toy. Little Katie had a vocabulary of only about 25 words, but "mine" was definitely one of them! As I stepped in to negotiate a cease-fire, I was made aware that the concept of stewardship and sharing did not come natural to them. It reinforced in my own mind the need for me, as their father, to role model that quality before them. I have since tried to demonstrate to them by actions and attitudes that God owns all things, and what I possess I possess as a responsible steward. I must give account to God.

_____

(My name)

What are some rights that I naturally tend to believe are exclusively mine that actually belong to God?

_____

_____

_____

In what way can I trust God more after knowing He has such exclusive rights to everything?

_____

_____

_____

To reinforce my trust in God as authority, I will pray:

> *"Lord Jesus, thank You for all that You have provided. You own all that I have. You are worthy of my trust because You possess all the rights to all I need. Thank You for providing me with everything I receive. Amen."*

For Further Reference

For an amplification of how God's authority is translated into "The Authority of the Believer," read *Understanding the Occult*, Appendix II, pp. 195-202.

GOD KNOWS IT ALL

A Quick Look Back

I've discovered a fundamental ingredient to trustworthiness – authority. Authority relates directly to ownership rights. And ownership gives me access to what is necessary to carry out my promise. Personally, I can't be trusted unless I have sufficient authorization to fulfill my word. By right of creation, God has the authority to move heaven and earth, if necessary, to carry out the promises of His Word. God owns everything. God can be trusted because He has the final authority.

———————————O———————————

Key Truth

God can be trusted because He is Infinite Wisdom, perceiving all of life accurately.

I will learn:

- how wisdom is seeing from God's viewpoint.
- how God's perspective is always accurate.
- how God sets the standard for interpreting life.

———————————O———————————

What Would You Say?

"I believe education is the key to solving man's problems. In this technological age of computers we are gathering vast amounts of understanding. Through educational advancements we will continue to make great strides in answering the many dilemmas facing man today. Knowledge gives us insight into the meaning of life."

What would *you* say?

I would say _____

_____

_____

Because _____

_____

_____

———————————O———————————

Let's Lay A Foundation

You should not trust someone simply because he has the authority to make his promise good. Authority can be abused. I suggest you add wisdom to your list of qualifications for trustworthiness. Wisdom guides the use of authority, enabling a person to know best how to fulfill a promise.

In business, it's common for colleagues to sign agreements that include a section entitled, "Full Understanding." By signing the agreement, each businessman acknowledges that he understands the contract. If a person is to be trusted, he must have a clear understanding of the promise he is making, and how it affects others.

If this is true of our interpersonal relationships, it is certainly true of our relationship with God. Can God be trusted? What does God's Word reveal about God's wisdom? What is there about God's wisdom that qualifies Him to be trusted?

The following scriptural words are often assumed to be synonymous. I think they have distinct meanings. I like to differentiate them in this way:

Knowledge has to do with *information*, the possession of facts and truths. *Understanding* has to do with *comprehension*, making knowledge useful by applying concepts. And *wisdom* has to do with *perception*, accurately judging the outcome of one's choices.

I. God perceives exhaustively.

God's wisdom is tied to His perception. He sees all of life with unlimited perception and knowledge. God sees the total picture, the whole panorama of reality at once. From His eternal viewpoint, God sees the end from the beginning.

1. God's wisdom is infinite.

God's attributes are qualities that are true only of God. God is holy, true, loving, righteous, faithful and merciful. He is also eternal, unchangeable, omnipresent, omnipotent, perfect, incomprehensible and omniscient. Each quality and attribute exists in God in perfect harmony. One does not exclude the other. No one attribute of God operates in isolation from the others. They all reside in perfect balance together.

God's wisdom does not exist apart from His infinity. What God knows, understands, and perceives is infinitely complete. Infinite insight belongs only to God. God's wisdom is immense.

"Great is our Lord, and abundant in strength; His _____

_____

_____" (Psalm 147:5).

God's knowledge and understanding are from two vantage points – eternity past and eternity future. He perceives all in His never-ending present.

"Before the mountains were born, or thou didst give birth to the earth

and the world, even from _____ to

_____, _____

_____" (Psalm 9:2).

Scripture asserts that God's attributes are affected by the qualities of His nature. God is both wise *and* infinite. If God is wise and God is infinite then God's wisdom is infinite. In contrast, man may be wise but never infinite.

Scripture depicts God's attributes as co-existent with God.

"The Lord _____ at the _____

_____, before _____. From

_____ I was established, from _____

_____, from the earliest times of the earth," (Proverbs 8:22-23).

To whom is Solomon referring?

Proverbs 8:12 – _____

2. God's wisdom is unfathomable.

Because God's wisdom *is* infinite, we can't comprehend it.

Wisdom that perceives the past, present and future is beyond our capabilities. Knowledge that encompasses the full spectrum of eternity is inconceivable to us.

What does King David acknowledge about God's knowledge of us?

"Such knowledge is _____

_____; it is _____

_____, I _____

_____ to it." (Psalm 139:6).

While we can't know everything there is to know about God, what we do know is true. In fact, we will have all of eternity to explore new dimensions of our relationship with God. God is unendlingly knowable. After ages in eternity, we still won't know all there is to know about God. Yet what little bit we do know, is true.

In reviewing God's end-of-the-age plan for Israel, Paul bursts out in eloquent praise of God's wisdom.

"Oh, the _____

_____ both of the wisdom and knowledge of God! How _____

_____ are His judgments and _____

_____ His ways!" (Romans 11:33).

II. God perceives accurately.

Did you ever see the Norman Rockwell painting of the little boy watching a baseball game through a knothole in the ballpark fence? The boy's line of eyesight is straight ahead. Anything to the side, or close to the fence is out of view. Yet, the spectators in the grandstands see the whole game. Our view of life is like that of the boy at the fence. It is extremely limited. We can't see the whole field. In contrast, God sees accurately because He sees fully. God has a panoramic, all-at-once view of life.

God's perception is both true and right.

1. God's view is always true.

God sees things as they truly are. God sees our lives in their true setting. What we see as the jumbled events of our lives, God sees as a part of His plan. He is never confused. He accurately perceives life as it actually exists. Nothing is hidden from God.

"And there is no creature _____

_____, but _____ and _____

_____

with whom we have to do" (Hebrews 5:13).

In Psalm 19 David distinguishes between God's view as true and God's view as right.

"The _____ of the Lord _____

_____; they are _____

_____" (Psalm 19:9).

Judgments are based upon one's perception of the facts. God's evaluation is always true because God sees the totality of life, the whole.

Because God's perception of life is true, how does the psalmist characterize God's Word, His commandments in Psalm 119?

Vs. 142 – _____

Vs. 151 – _____

Vs. 160 – _____

2. God's view is always right.

In addition to seeing what is truly there, God sets the standard for the right interpretation of what is there. My perspective is right only when it aligns with God's perspective.

So, God's evaluation of life is right because His view always adheres to His standard of rightness. That is the meaning of God's righteousness, God's character sets the standard for right. All God's ways adhere to His standard, they are right.

Therefore, God's perspective of things is always accurate. His precepts (guiding principles) are right.

"The _____ of the Lord are _____, rejoicing the heart" (Psalm 19:8).

66

Since God does all things right, how are His words and works affected?

Psalm 33:4 – _____

_____

_____

3. God's view is not always our view.

God's wisdom is both true and right. It follows that if we are to evaluate life truly and interpret life rightly, we must take God's view as our own. That is the meaning of true wisdom – seeing life from God's perspective. We have the choice to accept God's wisdom or reject it. As natural men we perceive very differently from God. We often reject God's evaluation of things.

"For _____

_____, neither are _____

_____, declares the Lord. For as the heavens are higher

than the earth, so are _____,

and _____

_____" (Isaiah 55:8-9).

The problem is not always a matter of rebellion against God's way. We need to be informed of God's view. Natural man simply perceives his way to be right and proceeds through life on that basis. Natural thought patterns blind us all. But God has communicated His view of life to us through His Word. It must become our new basis of evaluation.

How does the natural man, thinking on a human level, evaluate the ways of God?

1 Corinthians 2:14 – _____

_____

_____

Why can't he understand spiritual things?

1 Corinthians 2:14 – _____

_____

_____

How has every believer been equipped to change our basis of evaluation to God's viewpoint?

1 Corinthians 2:14 – _____

_____

_____

Conclusion

Wisdom is a necessary ingredient to the criteria of trustworthiness, accurately judging the outcome of one's choices. God has infinite wisdom, perceiving all of life accurately, qualifying Him to be trusted. Since God infinitely knows and perceives all things, He is capable of understanding how His claims are to be fulfilled. God can be trusted on the basis of His infinite wisdom.

————————O————————

Feedback

Multiple Choice

See the key at the end of this lesson.

_____1. A necessary ingredient for a person to be worthy of trust includes:
   A. Signing a contract witnessed by officers of the court.
   B. A clear understanding of the promise he is making and how that affects others.
   C. Having a co-signer.

_____2. God fully understands what He has promised and can be trusted because:
   A. All His promises have been recorded.
   B. His understanding is infinitely exhaustive and right.
   C. He has the capacity to evaluate logically.

_____3. When Scripture says God's wisdom is unfathomable it means:
   A. His wisdom is beyond our comprehension.
   B. His wisdom is not at all logical.
   C. His wisdom is not complete.

_____4. God's perception of life is always accurate because:
   A. Christians believe so.
   B. He created life and knows all about it.
   C. He sees the totality of life, the whole.

_____5. God's wisdom is not accepted by the natural man because:
   A. He doesn't think the way God thinks.
   B. He hasn't read the Bible enough.
   C. He hasn't obeyed all of God's law.

_____6. God's wisdom becomes our new basis of evaluation by:
   A. Thinking each decision through carefully.
   B. Seeking the opinions of good friends.
   C. Accepting God's view of life communicated through His Word.

————————O————————

My Response

Josh

Some time ago I was invited to the White House for a roundtable discussion concerning serious problems facing our nation. I listened for over an hour to the various solutions posed to deal with the problems. When asked to comment, I shared my perspective. I said, "Gentlemen, there are economic solutions for economic problems, political solutions for political problems and spiritual solutions to spiritual problems. I believe we are trying to propose a human solution to a spiritual problem."

One powerful government leader leaned over and said, "Mr. McDowell, I hope you're right. Our problems are beyond the power of government to solve."

I came away from that meeting convinced that natural man cannot perceive the answers to his problems because they are spritually discerned. I was reminded that acknowleging God as the solution is the beginning of wisdom.

_____

(My name)

What viewpoint have I had recently that appeared correct to me but I later found, through God's Word, that it was wrong?

_____

_____

_____

In what new way can I trust God after knowing He has such an accurate perception of life?

_____

_____

_____

To reinforce my trust in God as wisdom, I will pray:

"Father, I'm thankful You see me and my situation accurately. You're worthy of my trust because You are infinitely wise, seeing truly and right. You know all there is to know about me and yet You love me. Help me to learn Your ways of wisdom and walk in them. Amen."

For Further Reference

For a brief, analytical look at the attributes of God, read Chapter 3, "The Beliefs of Orthodox Christianity" in *Understanding the Cults*, pp. 31-50.

GOD'S POWER IS UNLIMITED

A Quick Look Back

I've added an additional quality to my growing list of qualifications for God's trustworthiness: wisdom. I've learned that God is infinitely wise, having complete understanding to know how to fulfill His promises. I'm safe trusting a God like that! God's wisdom qualifies Him to be trusted because He knows the course to follow to fulfill His Word. For me, true wisdom depends upon seeing life as God sees it. This becomes my new basis for evaluating life's experiences.

———————————O———————————

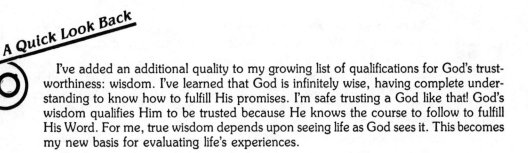

Key Truth

God can be trusted because He is all powerful, having the strength to accomplish all things.

I will learn:

- that God's power will never be depleted.
- where God's power originates.
- why the entire creation is dependent upon God's power.

———————————O———————————

What Would You Say?

"Within you is the potential to be anything you want to be. Inside you is an untapped reservoir of energy. Unleash it! Believe in yourself! Limitations are generally self-imposed. Draw on your inner strength and you'll be surprised what you can do."

What would *you* say?

I would say _____

_____

_____

Because _____

_____

_____

————————O————————

Let's Lay A Foundation

In this lesson we will investigate a third reason God is worthy of our trust – He is all-powerful. Another name for that attribute is omnipotence.

If someone is to be worthy of my trust, he must have the strength to accomplish what he promises. A person may be authorized, and possess an ingenious plan, but unless he has the strength to carry out his claim he is not fully trustworthy. Adequate power is necessary to fulfill a claim. God's power enables Him to keep His promises without fail.

This lesson may very well help to revolutionize your relationship with Christ. Consider once again why God is qualified to receive your trust.

I. God's Word defines God's power.

What we learn we often learn by contrast. God uses this technique to teach us what He is like. He compares familiar ideas with Himself, drawing parallels. God defines the greatness of His power by using illustrations we understand.

1. God's power is eternal.

Because God is eternal, His power is eternal. While that may appear obvious, it has significant implications. God has no deficiency of strength to fulfill His promises. His power will never fail.

Our world is extremely energy conscious. Many believe the future of modern civilization hinges on the wise use and development of energy. The entire 1982 World's Fair in Knoxville, Tennessee was devoted to the theme of energy. Our society is increasingly aware that our energy resources are limited.

God's power, however, is not subject to temporal laws. God's strength will never dissipate.

What does creation tell us about God's power?

Romans 1:20 – _____

Creation is limited in what it can tell us about God, yet it does demonstrate His eternal power.

How long will God rule by His power?

Psalm 66:7 – _____

God's Word shows us that God's power and might will never end. God's power is eternal because God is eternal.

2. God's power is absolute.

Nothing surpasses God's power. Think of the greatest exhibition of power imaginable, and God's power exceeds it! No other power can match God's power. It is above all others.

72

What name did the Lord Jesus use to describe Himself to the Apostle John?

Revelation 1:8; 22:13 – _____

_____

_____

That no doubt corresponds to an Old Testament name for God, El Shaddai, the Almighty. El Shaddai means that God's power supercedes all other power; nothing can keep God from accomplishing His objective.

What is a good example of the greatness of God's power?

Jeremiah 32:17 – _____

_____

_____

What distinguishes God's power from man's power, according to Luke 18:27 and Matthew 19:26?

_____

_____

_____

God is all-powerful, yet He can do nothing contrary to His holy nature. God cannot sin, for He is holy and righteous. It is impossible for God to deny His essential nature as God. Someone has said, "Power corrupts man. And absolute power corrupts absolutely." While that may be true of man, with God there is no corruption. While God has absolute power, He always uses it consistent with His divine nature. God has no restrictions on His absolute power except the inability to go against His own nature.

II. God is the source of all power.

Not only is God eternally powerful, but all power that exists is derived from Him. Power to accomplish anything comes from God.

1. God is self-dependent.

God generates His own power. God is totally self-sufficient, not dependent upon anyone for strength.

Paul shocked the scholarly world with this news.

"The God who made the world and all things in it, since He is the Lord of heaven and earth, does not dwell in temples, made with hands; neither

_____, as though _____

_____, since He Himself _____

_____ and

_____" (Acts 17:24-25).

2. Creation is dependent upon God's power.

73

As creatures created in God's image, what three things do we depend upon God for?

Acts 17:28 – 1)_____, 2)_____,

3)_____

The world is not a cosmic timepiece, wound up by God and left to run on its own. The universe depends upon God's constant attention. Everything in creation depends on God's sustaining power.

Two key passages reveal how God uses His power to remind us of our dependence on Him.

(1) *Colossians 1:16-17:*

"For by Him _____, both

in the heavens and on earth, visible and invisible, whether thrones

or dominions or rulers or authorities – all things have been _____

_____. And He is before all things, and in Him

_____

(2) *Hebrews 1:3:*

"And He is the radiance of His glory and the exact representa-

tion of His nature, and _____

_____ by the _____

_____. . ."

3. Believers are dependent upon God's power.

The Christian life is a supernatural life, lived by supernatural power. God gives His power to us so we can live an abundant life. This power is released in us by the filling of the Holy Spirit (Ephesians 5:18).

What does Paul pray would be the experience of every believer?

Ephesians 3:16 – _____

_____

_____

What is God's power able to do in our lives?

Acts 1:8 – _____

Ephesians 3:20 – _____

1 Peter 1:5 – _____

In another prayer for believers in the book of Ephesians, Paul clearly iden-tifies the power that is working in us.

74

That you may know. . .what is the_____

_____ toward us who believe. These are in accordance with _____

_____ which He brought about in Christ,

when _____, and _____

_____ in the heavenly places" (Ephesians 1:18-20).

This is the standard of God's power working in the Christian. The same power that raised Christ from the dead is the power working in us now.

What else will God use His power to do?

1 Corinthians 6:14 – _____

Conclusion

God's power qualifies Him to be trusted. Since God has the power to accomplish all things, His claims can be carried out. God can be trusted because of His unlimited power.

————————O————————

Feedback

True or false

See the key at the end of the lesson for correct answers.

____1.   To be fully trusted one must have the strength to accomplish what he promised.

____2.   God's power is eternal. He has no deficiency of strength to fulfill His promises.

____3.   God depends on other sources for power.

____4.   God created the world, giving it the capacity to be self-sustaining.

____5.   God's power has no restrictions other than the inability to go against His own nature.

What has God done in your life exceeding abundantly beyond what you ever asked or imagined? Briefly summarize what He did.

_____

_____

_____

————————O————————

My Response

Josh

Some time ago I visited a planetarium and was made aware of the awesome energy in our sun. Though 93 million miles away, its rays warm our planet. The sun generates heat by converting hydrogen into helium at the rate of 600 million metric tons a second, raising temperatures up to 15 million degrees! What an energy source! But this means that the sun is actually using up its store of energy. In approximately 5,000 million years, the hydrogen will be exhausted. Not that I'm concerned, but it made me realize that the sun will burn out one day. The only reliable source I can depend on never to lose power is my Heavenly Father – the Alpha and Omega – the Almighty! Christ is my sufficiency.

_____

(My name)

What new insight have I gained about God's power?

_____

_____

_____

I need to experience God's power in many areas of my life. The most important one right now is:

_____

_____

_____

To remind me to depend on God's power, I will pray:

> *"Lord, thank You for giving me power to do Your will. You are Almighty, the God with eternal power. Keep me from taking credit for what You accomplish in my life. I will continue to rely on You to live an abundant Christian life. Your power is all I need. I'm expecting great things ahead. Amen."*

For Further Reference

For a usable explanation of the Holy Spirit's ministry in a believer's life read Transferable Concepts 3 and 4, *How to be Filled with the Spirit* and *How to Walk in the Spirit*, by Bill Bright.

GOD CONTROLS EVERYTHING

A Quick Look Back

I've discovered the meaning of God's unlimited power, another reason God can be trusted. God's power is eternal – lasting forever, never depleting. And though God's power is absolute, He will never use it for corrupt purposes. Thus, God lacks no resource in fulfilling every promise He ever made. His power exceeds my broadest imagination. Practically, I experience God's power in my life through the filling of the Holy Spirit.

―――――――O―――――――

Key Truth

God can be trusted because He is absolute Controller, directing each situation to achieve His purpose.

I will learn:

- how God's purpose is accomplished through His absolute control.
- how God can guarantee that His purpose will be accomplished.
- how man's choices harmonize with God's control.

―――――――O―――――――

What Would You Say?

"I'm not an atheist; I just don't believe God manipulates events like a cosmic stage manager. God expects us to work out our own problems. I've observed that most people use God as a crutch. When they have a problem they think God will solve it. I always say, 'Take charge of your life; control your own destiny; or you won't get anywhere.'"

What would *you* say?

I would say _____

_____

_____

Because _____

_____

_____

———————————O———————————

Let's Lay A Foundation

Like most of you, I struggle to manage an already overloaded schedule. Since I work best under pressure, I welcome deadlines. They truly help me. Deadlines force me to be very conscious of time and avoid interruptions.

Sometimes though, try as I might, I miss a deadline. I want to accomplish the task; I see the steps I need to take to achieve the goal; I even have the motivation and energy to do it, but circumstances beyond my control rearrange my schedule. Travel delays, printing delays, postal delays – there are circumstances I just can't regulate.

So, I've learned not to promise what is beyond my control!

Strictly speaking, if someone is to be totally trusted, he must be able to direct circumstances to meet his purpose. That's the only way he can be trusted 100 percent. To be totally trustworthy, you must completely control circumstances.

Obviously, nobody claims to be 100 percent trustworthy – except God. God, though, commits Himself to fulfill every promise. To do that, God must be in absolute control of circumstances. Is that what the Bible says about God? Does He control circumstances so completely as to never miss on a promise?

I. God has an advance plan.

God is the master planner. Nothing catches Him by surprise. He prepares in advance for circumstances without a worry that things won't go as He planned.

When did God prepare the kingdom for His followers?

Matthew 25:34 – _____

When did God choose that we were to be in Christ?

"He chose us in Him _____
_____, that we should be holy and blameless before Him" (Ephesians 1:4).

In fact, man's sin did not catch God by surprise. While God gave man the freedom to obey or rebel, He knew the outcome. God already had a plan to reconcile and restore us to a love relationship. Love requires a choice. Love cannot be forced.

When did God conceive the plan of redemption?

2 Peter 1:18-20 – _____

II. God has a determined purpose.

Behind every plan is a purpose. God wills that His purpose be fulfilled. God's purpose is fixed. You can count on it.

What determines God's purpose?

Ephesians 1:11 – _____

What did God do to assure us He would never change His mind on a promise?

Hebrews 6:16-17_____

When God wills something, it will be done!

III. God's plan includes Christlikeness.

God's plan is that every believer become like His Son, Jesus Chirst. Salvation encompasses the total restoration of the universe, including the restoration of every believer to match the complete personhood of Jesus Christ.

1. Christlikeness is restoration.

   Being transformed into the image of Jesus is being restored to the original pattern God planned for us from creation.Through Christ we become truly fulfilled, whole persons.

   What did God choose that we would become in Christ?

   "For whom he foreknew, He also _____ to become

   _____, that He might be the first-born among many brethren." (Romans 8:29).

   God determined in advance that everyone who personally received Christ as Savior and Lord was destined to be holy, like His Son. Holiness means, among other things, wholeness. Through Christ, we are restored to authentic personhood. Sin brings alienation and discord, in us and others. Christ brings inward peace and harmony. Through Christ, the spiritual dimension of our lives is restored to wholeness. Ultimately, in final redemption, we will be fully restored in every dimension of our lives – spiritually, mentally, emotionally, and physically.

   What will we be transformed into?

   "Who will_____

   into _____, by the exertion of the power that He has even to subject all things to Himself" (Philippians 3:21).

   How is this restoration process accomplished?

   "But we all, with unveiled face_____

   the _____, are_____

   into _____ from _____, just as from the Lord, the Spirit" (2 Corinthians 3:18).

2. Christlikeness is the pattern.

   Christ is the head of a whole new race, the family of God. Being like Jesus means we take on the family likeness. Consistent with our new status in God's family is the stamp of family identity.

   Look again at Romans 8:29:

   "For whom He foreknew, He also predestined to become

   _____, that He might be _____

   _____."

Christ becomes the pattern for a new race of humanity. He stands as the first, the head of eternity's new race. In Christ, I have a new identity.

IV. God's plan cannot be changed.

God can be fully trusted because His plans are never altered by circumstances. From our human perspective, God is faced with innumerable obstacles to achieving His purpose. God chooses, however, to use the very circumstances that appear to defeat His plan to accomplish His plan.

1. God always overcomes opposition.

Because God's purpose is unchanging, nothing can prohibit Him from accomplishing His ultimate goal. He is in complete control no matter what the resistance. In fact, God is in such control that oppositon will never defeat God's purpose.

"I know that Thou _____ _____

_____, and that no purpose of Thine _____

_____" (Job 42:1).

While God has given us freedom to make many choices in our lives, our choices will never thwart God's purposes. How does man's freedom harmonize with God's sovereignty?

Consider these two observations:

(1) Man's freedom of choice was given by God.

(2) Man's sphere of freedom is limited.

This concept can be visualized this way:

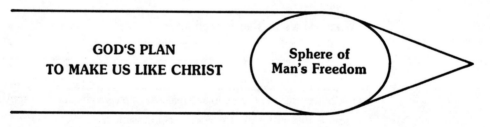

GOD'S PLAN TO MAKE US LIKE CHRIST

Sphere of Man's Freedom

Man's choices never keep God from achieving His ultimate goals. Man's freedom will always be exercised within the boundaries set by God. Man is truly free but only in a limited sphere.

2. God transforms oppositon into assistance.

What are obstacles to us are actually building blocks to God. The thing that would appear to defeat His purpose, He uses to aid His purpose. That is the meaning of Psalm 76:10:

"For the _____ shall _____; with a remnant of wrath Thou shalt gird Thyself."

An example of this is Adam's fall into sin. Adam's sin would appear on the surface to wreck God's plan to create us for fellowship with Him and to rule His creation. Redemption is God's plan to restore this present world order to a better-than-original state. What Satan thought would decisively defeat God, God used to accomplish His plan anyway.

Yet, many times circumstances *appear* to interfere with God's purpose for our lives. God allows difficulties to come, and we are faced with trials, problems and at times, serious conflicts. But has God lost control?

Based on Romans 8:28:

(1) What does God cause all things to do?

_____

(2) Who is working these things together for our good?

_____

(3) Who are those people that God works for?

_____

From Romans 8:29, what specific good does God have in mind for us?

_____

Conclusion

God has absolute control to direct every situation to achieve His purpose, qualifying Him to be trusted. Since God has the ability to regulate every situation, His claims can be fulfilled. God can be trusted on the basis of His absolute control.

Feedback

True or false

See the key at the end of the lesson for answers.

____1. Only God can guarantee His promises. He alone has absolute control over life.

____2. A relationship with Christ restores the spiritual dimension of our lives. In final redemption, we will be fully restored spiritually, mentally, emotionally, physically.

____3. It took God approximately 4000 years after creating man to conceive of redemption and reconciliation.

____4. Although every Christian faces problems, even serious setbacks, God still accomplishes His purpose to make us like Christ.

____5. God can be fully trusted because God's plans are never changed by circumstances.

____6. Man's choices harmonize with God's control by:
(1) being given by God.
(2) being exercised within the boundaries set by God.

My Response

Josh

In my first year of college I decided on a law career. But that was only a stepping stone. Over a period of weeks I developed goals, specific objectives and a detailed plan of implementation. I mapped out a 25-year plan to become governor of Michigan. The plan was in 50 six-month periods. This was no fantasy to me. I saw it as a realistic goal. The main barrier to my fulfilling the plan was that I left out God's will and purpose for my life. I've never become governor of Michigan. He changed my plans. I learned though, that God uses the smallest details of my life to accomplish His plan. I find great motivation and fulfillment when my plans align with God's purpose for my life.

_____
(My name)

What difficult situation do I face that I want God to deal with? (check one)

_____ family problem	_____ time management problem
_____ financial problem	_____ procrastination
_____ career (school) problem	_____ worry
_____ major decision	_____ low self-image

I will bring that problem before God now, knowing He can deal with it. Here is my need:

_____

_____

_____

To reinforce my trust in God as controller, I will pray:

"Lord, thank You for being the absolute controller of my life. You have a master plan for my life which includes being conformed to the likeness of Your Son. I submit to Your control to achieve that plan. You are worthy of my trust because You direct every situation of my life to achieve Your purpose. Help me to be alert to the ways you take to complete that plan. Amen."

————————O————————

For Further Reference

For examples of God's control of circumstances, read these incidents of Josh's life in *Josh, The Excitement of the Unexpected*, pp. 79-82 and 123-141.

Key
1. T, 2. T, 3. F, 4. T, 5. T, 6. T

Section 3

GOD CAN BE TRUSTED: EVIDENCE OF TRUSTWORTHINESS

ABRAHAM: YIELDING TO GOD'S AUTHORITY

A Quick Look Back

I've learned that God is qualified to be trusted because He is the final authority, possessing exclusive rights to creation; infinite wisdom, perceiving all of life accurately; ultimate power, having the strength to accomplish His will; absolute control, directing all of life to achieve His purpose.

God deserves my complete trust!

———————O———————

Key Truth

Trust in God's authority is evidenced through the life of Abraham.

I will learn:

- how Abraham responded to God's test.
- that God's authority is the basis of His trustworthiness.
- how trusting God creates contentment.

———————O———————

What Would You Say?

"I believe the only way people will respect you is to demand what's coming to you. Most people wll trample right over you. I say you've got to shove back. I don't want to hurt anybody, but I do want what rightfully belongs to me. In this world you have to fight for what you get; nobody will roll over and play dead."

What would *you* say?

I would say _____

_____

_____

Because _____

_____

_____

—————————————O——————————

Let's Lay A Foundation

Authority is a scary word. Many people think authority stifles and restricts our creativity. Actually the opposite is true. Freedom is discovered through the protection of authority. Authority is not always negative. There are many positive benefits to being under authority.

Authority doesn't mean dictatorship; it means responsible ownership. In this lesson, which correlates with Lesson 6, we will learn how Abraham discovered God to be totally trustworthy, based on God's ultimate authority. Through Abraham's life we gain an insight into God's character, His proven dependability.

I. Abraham demonstrates trust in God's authority.

Abraham demonstrates a remarkable kind of faith. Abraham did not have the full revelation about God that we have in our completed Bible. Abraham had no Bible at all! Nonetheless, he responded in faith to God, demonstrating his confidence in God's choices for his life.

1. Abraham's response to God's call.

Abraham is a classic Old Testament example of a man responding to God's authority. He believed God owned all, qualifying God to fulfill what He promised.

What did God call Abraham to do?

Genesis 12:1 – _____

_____

_____

Did Abraham know where he was to go?

Genesis 12:1 – _____

How did Abraham respond to God's call?

"By _____ Abraham, when he was called _____

_____ which he was

to receive for an inheritance; and _____

_____, _____

where he was going" (Hebrews 11:8).

2. Abraham's response to God's promise.

Incorporated into God's call was God's promise. With the command, came God's provision.

Note three aspects of God's promise to Abraham in Genesis 12:1-2. "Go forth"

(1) *A land* – "To the _____ which _____

_____" (vs. 1).

(2) *An heir* – "And I will make you a _____" (vs. 2).

(3) *A blessing* – "And I will _____" (vs. 2).

Abraham personally received honor, wealth and prominence (Genesis 13:2,6). But God's promised blessing was to extend beyond Abraham. Central to the fulfillment of God's promise was the provision for an heir. Through an heir would come possession of a land and the bestowal of a blessing to the earth.

Embedded in God's promise to Abraham of an heir is an added spiritual dimension. God's original promise to Abraham encompassed more than the birth of Isaac. A spiritual blessing was to come to the whole world through the Messiah, Jesus Christ (Galatians 3:16).

God's original promise to Abraham encompased more than the birth of Isaac. A spiritual blessing was to come to the whole world through the Messiah, Jesus Christ.

Did Abraham believe God could fulfill His Word? What was his response to God's promise?

Genesis 15:6 – _____

3. Abraham's response to God's test.

What a learning process for Abraham to wait for God to fulfill His promise! The day came (Abraham was old) for Isaac to be born. Isaac symbolized God's commitment to fulfill all His promises (Genesis 21:12).

Abraham had attempted to fulfill God's promises by himself. Repeatedly, God reminded Abraham that the promise was a gift, owned by God, to be fulfilled on God's timetable. God reinforced this point by waiting until Abraham and Sarah were beyond child-bearing years, making it necessary to reverse a naturally hopeless condition to fulfill the promise. God made unmistakably clear that He alone possessed the right to fulfill the promise, on His timetable. In the process, God stripped Abraham of all dependence on human achievement. Now, God takes him a step further.

What did God ask Abraham to do with Isaac, the son of promise?

Genesis 22:1-2 – _____

_____

_____

How puzzled Abraham must have been! Child sacrifices were commonplace in pagan religions, and Yahweh condemned such practices. Yet, judging from Abraham's perspective, God was asking him to murder his son, thereby destroying the son of promise, dashing hope of any fulfillment.

God required Abraham to yield the right granted him by God to have a nation through Isaac. God had promised, yet God tested Abraham's submission to God's authority.

The significance of Abraham's obedience is summarized in Hebrews 11:17-18:

"By _____, when he was tested,

_____; and _____ who had

_____ was _____

it was _____,

_____;

'In Isaac your descendents shall be called.'"

Abraham obeyed God. Abraham believed God had the right to choose how the promise was to be fulfilled. Abraham yielded his right to a son to God, believing God would still keep His promise.

II. Abraham benefits from trust in God's authority.

God kept Abraham from sacrificing Isaac, knowing Abraham's willingness to obey Him in every way. God returned as a gift what Abraham was willing to sacrifice.

1. The sacrifice was replaced.

What did Abraham use as a sacrifice in place of his son?

Genesis 22:13 – _____

What name did Abraham call the place?

Genesis 22:14 – _____

The burnt offering denotes a sacrifice of dedication and praise. Abraham perceived that God, in the position of authority, longs to provide all our needs. No doubt Abraham reaffirmed God's ownership of all things, qualifying Him always to keep His Word.

2. The sacrifice was returned.

In Abraham's mind, Isaac was as good as gone! God honored Abraham by returning what he yielded to God. God will often return as a gift the rights we freely yield.

How did God respond to Abraham's obedience?

"By _____

_____, declares the Lord, because you have _____

_____, and have not _____

_____, _____, indeed I

will_____, and I

will _____ as the stars
of the heavens" (Genesis 22:16-17).

According to Genesis 22:18, what was the reason God promised to provide so for Abraham?

_____

In what way did God bless and provide for Abraham?

Genesis 24:1 – _____

III. The result of trusting God's authority.

1. Abraham experienced contentment.

   Abraham yielded his rights to God because he believed God owned them anyway. God asked Abraham to yield what God had promised him for years. Abraham made no demands on how God was to fulfill His promise. He obeyed, yielded to God's authority and discovered deep joy and contentment.

   At the close of Abraham's life, how does Genesis 25:8 characterize him?

   _____

   _____

   _____

2. We can experience contentment.

   The key to contentment is in yielding one's rights to God. I transfer to God the ownership of those things I consider valuable. God is more capable of protecting what belongs to Him than I am. Contentment is a quality that results from trust in God's authority.

   What is God's plan for contentment?

   (1) Reject false security.

   "Let your character be free from the love of money, _____

   _____; for He Himself has said,

   _____, nor

   _____,'" (Hebrews 13:5).

   (2) Commit your needs to God.

   "Be anxious for nothing, but in _____ by

   _____ and _____ with _____

   _____ let _____. And the _____

   which _____ shall _____

   and _____ in Christ Jesus" (Philippians 4:6-7).

(3) Accept God's provision.

"Not that I speak from want; for I have _____

_____ in _____

_____" (Philippians 4:11).

Conclusion

God demonstrates through the life of Abraham that He is trustworthy, fulfilling all His promises. God promised Abraham a land, a nation and a blessing. At God's command, he yielded ownership of his son to God, knowing that God would provide. He did. The evidence from the life of Abraham confirms God is trustworthy. When we place our trust in God, the one sufficiently authorized to fulfill His promises, we are truly contented.

───────────O───────────

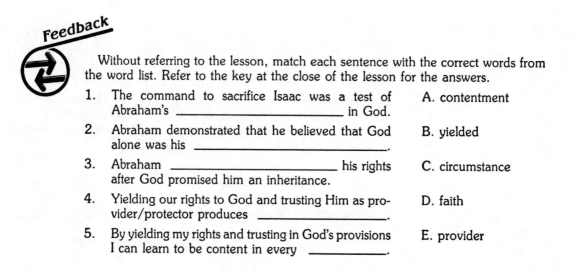

Feedback

Without referring to the lesson, match each sentence with the correct words from the word list. Refer to the key at the close of the lesson for the answers.

1. The command to sacrifice Isaac was a test of Abraham's _____ in God.

   A. contentment

2. Abraham demonstrated that he believed that God alone was his _____.

   B. yielded

3. Abraham _____ his rights after God promised him an inheritance.

   C. circumstance

4. Yielding our rights to God and trusting Him as provider/protector produces _____.

   D. faith

5. By yielding my rights and trusting in God's provisions I can learn to be content in every _____.

   E. provider

───────────O───────────

My Response

Josh

In my early years of marriage, I struggled with learning how to meet my wife's needs. No matter how much I told Dottie she was the most important person in my life, she didn't really feel it. I made a decision. I would yield some "Isaacs" – what I thought were legitimate, necessary ministry activities. It was hard at first. But in the long run I gained much more. Not only did I encourage my wife, who now *knows* she is important to me, I gained a greater freedom. Because Dottie knows I enjoy other activities, she encourages me to do them. Yielding the rights I assumed were mine produced a better relationship with my wife, a greater freedom and an inner contentment knowing God's will is best for me.

_____

(My name)

Isaac was certainly special to his father. What is most special to me? (check one)

_____ husband   _____ friend

_____ wife   _____ car

_____ father   _____ occupation

_____ mother   _____ house

_____ son   _____ other_____

_____ daughter

Am I willing to sacrifice obediently that most important, even legitimate possession to God?

_____

Why not pray and thank God for this Isaac experience in your life.

"Lord Jesus, _____

_____

_____. Amen."

DANIEL: ACKNOWLEDGING GOD'S WISDOM

A Quick Look Back

I've learned from the life of Abraham the value of submitting to God's authority. Because God owns all things, He possesses rights to all things. As in the example of Abraham, even God's promises to me are fulfilled in God's time. I know God can be fully trusted because He has final authority over all things, accomplishing His will at His command.

———O———

Key Truth

Trust in God's wisdom is evidenced through the life of Daniel.

I will learn:

- that Daniel acknowledged God as his source of wisdom.
- that God is honored when we depend on His wisdom.
- that trusting in God's wisdom creates a teachable attitude.

———O———

What Would You Say?

"I don't know who people think they are! I've been doing this job for ten years. Now they bring in a young kid over me straight out of college, to rearrange our production system. This kid doesn't know the first thing about practical work, yet they expect me to listen to him. I know more about this job than that kid will ever know. Why, I perfected our present system when he was in grade school. I'm not unwilling to learn, but give me somebody who knows something!"

What would _you_ say?

I would say _____

_____

_____

Because _____

_____

_____

————————————O————————

Let's Lay A Foundation

The Bible has a great deal to say about godly wisdom. And no biblical character exemplifies this quality like Daniel. In this lesson, which corresponds with Lesson 7, we will follow Daniel in his pursuit of true wisdom.

God promises wisdom to each of us if we only ask. You will be encouraged as you follow Daniel's pattern for acquiring God's wisdom.

Record God's promise of wisdom for your life. Daniel's life is proof that God keeps His promise.

"But if any of you _____, let him_____

_____, who _____ and _____, and _____

_____" (James 1:5).

While Daniel did not have this New Testament promise to encourage his faith, the truth it expresses harmonizes perfectly with Daniel's experience.

I. Daniel's test.

Daniel, a devout Jew, was deported by King Nebuchadnezzar from Judah to Babylon just before the final fall of Judah to Persia in 586 B.C. He accompanied many other noblemen into forced exile (Daniel 1:1-4). He quickly distinguished himself as a young man of outstanding intelligence and wisdom. He was recruited to serve King Nebuchadnezzar as a personal advisor (Daniel 1:17-21).

A complex problem soon developed that tested Daniel's trust in God as his source of his wisdom. The king required something that set the resident wise men reeling in fear!

What two things did the king ask for?

(1) "Therefore tell me _____,

(2) that I may know that you can_____

_____" (Daniel 2:9).

The King wanted an interpretation without telling the dream! The Chaldean wise men had to know both the dream and the interpretation. Nebuchadnezzer wasn't about to be fooled by a fancy interpretation. If the interpreter knew the dream without being told it, Nebuchadnezzer reasoned that the interpretation would be accurate.

How difficult did the court astrologers consider this task to be?

Daniel 2:10 – _____

Who did they believe were the only ones capable of solving the mystery?

Daniel 2:11 _____

The king responded to the court astrologer's delay tactics by decreeing death for the entire group. Daniel and his friends were among those to be killed (Daniel 2:13).

2. Daniel's source of wisdom.

Daniel put himself on the line. Daniel immediately requested an appointment with the king to interpret the dream. He did not know the answer to the mystery but he was confident he knew where to find it.

What was Daniel's solution to this dilemma? What first step did Daniel and his friends take to solve the mystery?

Daniel 2:18 – _____

Daniel did not rely on his own understanding to explain the dream, as if he had the resource in himself. He was soon to go before the king, and he didn't have the answer.

God answered Daniel's prayer and revealed the solution to Daniel while he slept. When he awoke, Daniel praised God.

To whom, according to Daniel, does wisdom belong?

"Let _____ be blessed forever

and ever, for _____

_____" (Daniel 2:20).

What does Daniel declare about God's wisdom (Daniel 2:21-22)?

(1) What two things does God give (verse 21)?

1 _____

2. _____

(2) What does God reveal (verse 22)?

_____

_____

_____

Armed with God's revelation, Daniel went before the king. He prefaced his declaration and interpretation of the dream with a clear explanation of the source of his wisdom.

From whom did Daniel receive the answer to King Nebuchadnezzer's mystery?

Daniel 2:28 – _____

    Daniel had the chance to take credit for his insight into the king's dream. How much wisdom did Daniel personally claim to have?

Daniel 2:30 – _____

    Daniel asked for God's wisdom, and God gave it. Wisdom is seeing life from God's vantage point and being able to accurately discern the results of one's choices. Daniel's interpretation gave the king insight into God's plan for the future.

II. Daniel benefited from trusting God's wisdom.

1. Daniel's life was spared.

    Daniel faced a difficult problem: if he couldn't declare the mystery, he and his friends would die. What happened when Daniel depended on God trusting in God's wisdom? What did Daniel testify God gave him?

    "To Thee, O God of my fathers, I give thanks and praise, for _____

_____;

even now _____,
For Thou hast made known to us the king's matter" (Daniel 2:23).

    An evident benefit of Daniel receiving God's wisdom to interpret the king's dream was life – for himself and all the wise men of Babylon. Their lives were spared.

2. Daniel was promoted.

    To what level of government was Daniel promoted as a result of his knowledge and wisdom?

    "Then the king promoted Daniel and gave him many great gifts, and he

made him_____

_____ and _____

_____" (Daniel 2:48).

III. The result of trusting God's wisdom.

1. Daniel cultivated a teachable spirit.

    At the close of Daniel's interpretation, what was the king's response?

Daniel 2:46 – _____

    It would appear the king was struck with Daniel's ability, giving him all the credit. What affect did Daniel's performance have on the king's opinion of Daniel's God?

    "The king answered Daniel and said, 'Surely_____

_____ and _____

_____ and _____,
since you have been able to reveal this mystery'" (Daniel 2:47).

Interestingly, while Daniel was seen as the one making the interpretation, God was still honored. Daniel was careful to point out that wisdom did not originate from him, but from God. It was *God's* wisdom.

Acknowledging God's wisdom is the first step to being teachable. If Daniel had been confident of his own insight, he no doubt would have lost his life – and the other wise men would have lost their lives, too. Daniel was willing to be taught God's wisdom, permitting God to receive the glory. God honored all Daniel did because he relied not on his own limited understanding, but on God's infinite perception. Similarly, God will fulfill His promise to give us wisdom when we resolve to submit to God's instruction.

2. Godly wisdom produces teachability.

Most of us don't like "know-it-alls." They can be pretty obnoxious at times. But there is one who does know it all. And rather than parade His knowledge, He wants to share it with us – if we're willing to learn. When we truly believe God knows all, we completely change our view of ourselves and others.

(1) Man's wisdom.

Human wisdom is based on natural perceptions. Human wisdom evaluates everything from a man-centered perspective. Human wisdom produces pride.

What does self-centered knowledge produce? How much does a person actually know when he thinks he is knowledgeable?

"Knowledge makes _____, but love _____

_____. If anyone supposes that he knows anything, _____

_____" (1 Corinthians 8:1-2).

(2) God's wisdom.

What is God's standard of human relationships? How are we to relate to others?

"Rejoice _____, and weep _____

_____. Be of the _____

_____; do not be _____, but _____

_____. Do not be _____

_____" (Romans 12:15-16).

Human wisdom sows seeds of personal destruction, while godly wisdom produces righteousness. What eight ingredients of godly wisdom are listed in James 3:17?

"But the wisdom from above is"

1. _____

2. _____

3. _____

4. _____

5. _____

6. _____

7. _____

8. _____

Whom does God help? Whom does He oppose?

1 Peter 5:5 – _____

_____

_____

Conclusion

Based on Daniel's experience, God can be trusted. God keeps his promise to give wisdom to those who ask, and Daniel is an example of that principle. The evidence from Daniel's life confirms God is trustworthy. Daniel acknowledged God as his only source of wisdom, demonstrating a teachable heart. Teachability results in those who equally look to God as their only source of wisdom.

————————O————————

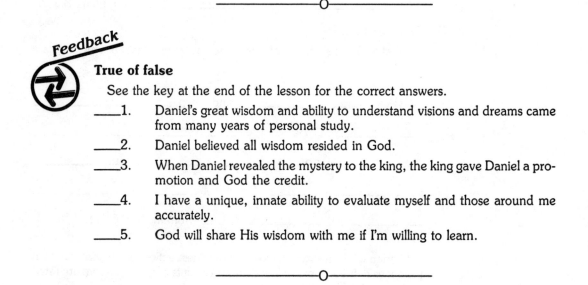

Feedback

True of false

See the key at the end of the lesson for the correct answers.

____1. Daniel's great wisdom and ability to understand visions and dreams came from many years of personal study.

____2. Daniel believed all wisdom resided in God.

____3. When Daniel revealed the mystery to the king, the king gave Daniel a promotion and God the credit.

____4. I have a unique, innate ability to evaluate myself and those around me accurately.

____5. God will share His wisdom with me if I'm willing to learn.

————————O————————

My Response

Josh

I used to think that the truly fulfilled people were the educated, intellectual people. I wasn't at the university long before I learned that my professors had more problems than I had. They could tell me how to make a better living, but they couldn't tell me how to live better. I found that pursuing academics did not meet my needs. It was only as I came to know Christ that I came to know the answers to life's questions – Who am I? Why am I here? Where am I going? Over these years I find the more I learn from God, the more I realize how little I really know.

_____

(My name)

Acknowledging my need for God's wisdom, I will describe a major problem in my life as clearly as I see it.

_____

_____

_____

Now, I'll rewrite the problem from God's viewpoint.

_____

_____

_____

By faith, I will pray:

> *"Lord Jesus, thank You for being my teacher. You see all of life accurately and know the solution to every problem. Help me always to trust in You, following Your ways. Many times, contrary to my natural way of thinking, insights to life come from the least expected person. Create in me a teachable spirit. Amen."*

GIDEON: DEPENDING ON GOD'S POWER

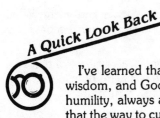

A Quick Look Back

I've learned that God can be trusted because of His wisdom. Daniel sought God's wisdom, and God gave it, fulfilling His promise. Daniel is an outstanding example of humility, always acknowledging that wisdom belonged not to him, but to God. I see that the way to cultivate a teachable spirit is to rely on God's wisdom, and to be willing to receive God's instruction even from those closest to me.

—————————O—————————

Key Truth

Trust in God's power is evidenced through the life of Gideon.

I will learn:

- what Gideon depended upon as his strength.
- what Gideon's trust in God accomplished.
- what is the key to personal strength and accomplishment.

—————————O—————————

What Would You Say?

"The secret to fulfilled living is cultivating your talents until you feel confident in yourself. Train yourself to be a quality person. Leaders develop their potential. Those who choose to succeed will succeed!"

What would *you* say?

I would say _____

_____

_____

Because _____

_____

_____

———————————————O———————————

The Bible is full of references to God's being our strength, power and might. What practical benefit does that have in our life? How does God's strength become our strength?

Gideon demonstrates how to turn God's power into a practical resource of personal power. In this lesson, which corresponds to Lesson 8, we will learn how Gideon put God's power to the test. I think you'll be challenged by the results.

God promises strength for weakness. Can God's promise be trusted? Gideon is a perfect example of God fulfilling His Word:

"He gives _____ to the _____, and to him who _____

_____ He _____" (Isaiah 40:29).

While Gideon did not have this word of encouragement from Isaiah, he found God to be his ultimate resource of power.

I. Gideon demonstrates trust in God's power.

The story of Gideon is a familiar one. Gideon needed strength to accomplish God's task. How did Gideon find such strength? What was his key to victory?

1. Gideon confirms God's power.

God promised to empower Gideon to defeat the enemy. Gideon was uncertain at first. He wanted to be sure God could be trusted.

There are two ways to determine a person's trustworthiness:

(1) By past record.

Gideon reflected on God's faithfulness to Israel in the past. What was his conclusion? Do you agree?

Judges 6:13 – _____

(2) By present reality.

Gideon was still reluctant to believe that God's past record of faithfulness related to him. Gideon wanted additional evidence of God's intention – confirmation that God would go with him to defeat Midian. Gideon wanted assurance that God would keep His Word, not guidance concerning God's will. Gideon knew what he was to do – fight Midian. He simply wanted to be sure God would keep His part of the bargain.

102

Describe the tests Gideon used to confirm God's promise.

"That Thou wilt deliver Israel through me, as Thou hast spoken."

Confirming test 1 (Judges 6:37-38) _____

_____

_____

Confirming test 2 (Judges 6:39-40) _____

_____

_____

God did not chide Gideon for his unbelief. Actually, God welcomed the opportunity to assure Gideon of His trustworthiness. Through the fleece, God pledged to Gideon to keep His promise.

Today we have a complete record in the Bible of God's acts in history, confirming God's trustworthiness. But that's not all.

What has God given each believer, personally, as God's pledge to always fulfill His promises?

"Now He who establishes us with you in Christ and anointed us is God,

who also _____

and gave us _____

_____" (2 Corinthians 1:21-22).

The Holy Spirit is God's "fleece," a pledge that God's promises are true.

2. God confirms Gideon's weakness.

God did not choose Gideon because of his great battlefield experience. In fact, Gideon's sense of inadequacy was the very thing that qualified him. In order for God to work powerfully through Gideon, He had to be sure Gideon was depending upon the *God* of Israel, not the *army* or Israel.

What danger did Israel face if they fought the battle with the original 32,000-member army?

"The people who are with you are too many for Me to give Midian into

their hands, lest _____,

saying, '_____

_____'" (Judges 7:2).

God was progressively weaning Gideon from dependence on human resources. God took away what seemed to be Gideon's only means of victory!

Gideon started out with an army of 32,000. After the first test, how many remained?

Judges 7:3 – _____

God said, "The people are still too many" (Judges 7:4). Following the second test, how many were left?

Judges 7:8 – _____

Gideon and his men faced overwhelming odds. The Midianites had 135,000 swordsmen (Judges 8:10). Yet, what was Gideon's challenge to his men?

"He returned to the camp of Israel and said, '_____

_____

_____'" (Judges 7:15).

II. Israel benefits from Gideon's trust in God's power.

1. The enemy was defeated.

What took place within the whole Midian army?

Judges 7:22 – _____

2. The land was recaptured.

"So Midian was subdued before the sons of Israel, and they did not lift

up their heads anymore. And _____

for _____

in the days of Gideon" (Judges 8:28).

3. God was honored.

The focus of Israel's attention was on Gideon for his valiant leadership. They wanted him to become their ruler. What was Gideon's response?

Judges 8:23 – _____

III. The result of trusting God's power.

1. We receive strength from God.

This is Paul's prayer for all believers:

"That you may be...strengthened with_____,

according to _____, for the

attaining of_____" (Colossians 1:11).

Many think that feelings of inadequacy and low self-esteem are the epidemic problem of the 20th century. Ultimately, what is God's answer?

"Not that we are_____ to

consider _____,

but _____" (2 Corinthians 3:5).

We are adequate to live a full life as we find our resource of strength in God.

2. Our weakness creates dependence.

One might think that acknowledging inadequacy is self-defeating. That is true if one wants to be independently strong. But we have weakness for a purpose. What is the purpose for our weakness?

"But we have this treasure in earthen vessels, that the surpassing great-

ness of the power _____"
(2 Corinthians 4:7).

How is power perfected?

2 Corinthians 12:9 – _____

_____

What should my attitude be about my weaknesses?

"Most gladly, therefore, _____

_____, that _____

_____" (2 Corinthians 12:9).

3. Our dependence creates strength.

Wouldn't boasting about my weaknesses, focusing on my inadequacies, create a gigantic inferiority complex?

Write out Philippians 4:13:

_____

_____

_____

Does that sound like inferiority? Paul's declaration was a shout of confidence – not in himself, but in Christ! It is vital to capitalize on the words "through Him." We don't succeed by our own efforts. The Christian life is not a self-help program. We don't succeed even by our weakness becoming strong through Christ. It is Christ using our weakness as an avenue to display His strength.

What was Paul content with? Why?

2 Corinthians 12:10 – _____

_____

_____

Paul's weakness forced him to depend upon God's strength. When I recognize my weakness, I can realize God's strength!

Conclusion

The record of Gideon's life is evidence that God can be trusted because of His power. God is able to accomplish what He promises. God kept His promise to Gideon enabling him to defeat the enemy. When we recognize our weakness, and depend upon God's power, God exercises His strength through us.

———————O———————

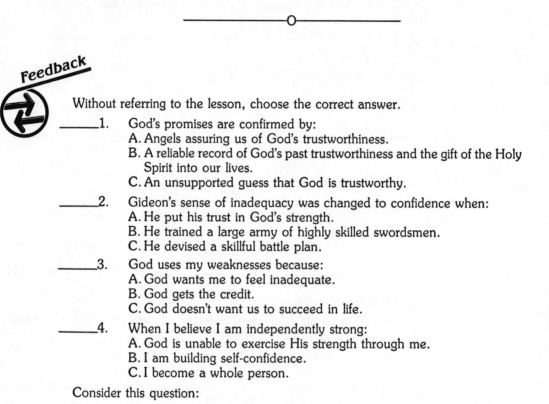

Feedback

Without referring to the lesson, choose the correct answer.

_____1.　God's promises are confirmed by:
　　　A. Angels assuring us of God's trustworthiness.
　　　B. A reliable record of God's past trustworthiness and the gift of the Holy Spirit into our lives.
　　　C. An unsupported guess that God is trustworthy.

_____2.　Gideon's sense of inadequacy was changed to confidence when:
　　　A. He put his trust in God's strength.
　　　B. He trained a large army of highly skilled swordsmen.
　　　C. He devised a skillful battle plan.

_____3.　God uses my weaknesses because:
　　　A. God wants me to feel inadequate.
　　　B. God gets the credit.
　　　C. God doesn't want us to succeed in life.

_____4.　When I believe I am independently strong:
　　　A. God is unable to exercise His strength through me.
　　　B. I am building self-confidence.
　　　C. I become a whole person.

Consider this question:

Do we need to put out "fleeces" today? Hasn't God already given us His "fleece," the Holy Spirit, assuring us He will always keep His Word?

_____

_____

_____

———————O———————

My Response

Josh

There came a time in my ministry when I knew I couldn't build my ministry alone. I had to have the help of others to carry out the vision of my ministry. I was limited. Soon, the entire effectiveness of my ministry was at stake. I prayed, "Lord, help me not to step out into a new venture without the confirmation of someone else's convic-

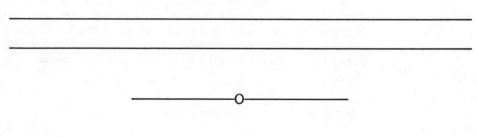

106

tions." I took two steps. First I admitted I couldn't do it alone, and second, I waited for the people God wanted to use to develop any new area of ministry.

It's become a rule of thumb with me now. I'll not move into a new area of ministry until God sends someone else along who has the same conviction I do and the ability to carry it out.

_____

(My name)

Based on Philippians 4:13, complete this sentence: I can do all things through Christ, including

_____

_____

_____

To encourage me to trust in God's power, I will pray:

> *"Lord Jesus, thank You for being everything I need. You're my strength. Help me to be content with my weakness so I can magnify Your strength. Teach me to depend upon You daily, so that Your strength can be channeled through my weakness. Amen."*

For Further Reference

For the story of how God expanded Josh's ministry through others, read *Josh, the Excitement of the Unexpected*, pp. 179-192.

JOB: SUBMITTING TO GOD'S CONTROL

A Quick Look Back

I've learned, through the life of Gideon, that God can be counted on to keep His Word, having the power to fulfill His purpose. This teaches me that God often chooses the least expected way to show Himself great. As a result I see that no one can boast in his own achievements, but everyone must trust in God's strength. Gideon depended on God's might to fight his battle, leading a band of 300 men to defeat an army many times its size. Gideon is an example of a man who trusted God for strength, and God proved Himself worthy of that trust. I know I can trust God fully because He alone has the power to carry out His desires perfectly.

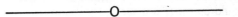

Key Truth

Trust in God's control is evidenced through the life of Job.

I will learn:

- how Job responded to tragedy.
- that God's control is the basis of His trustworthiness.
- how trusting God creates a sense of purpose.

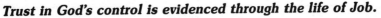

What Would You Say?

"I just don't understand. Life sure has its share of puzzles. I don't understand why some things happen. I guess it's just fate. If God was a good God, like some say, it seems He would do something about all the suffering and pain in the world."

What would *you* say?

I would say _____

_____

_____

Because _____

_____

_____

———————————O———————————

The life of Job gives us an insight into the meaning of difficulties and God's control over them. In this lesson, which correlates with Lesson 9, we will learn how Job discovered God to be trustworthy, based on His absolute control.

Many face some of the same problems as Job. Most, however, have never experienced the same amount of tragedies over such a short period of time. How did Job respond? What did he discover about God's control?

I. Job's response to God when he encountered tragedy.

Job was a blameless, upright and God-fearing man, but that did not isolate him from tragedy. In one single day his servants were murdered, his livestock was destroyed and all his children were killed. Later, Job's entire body was stricken with sores.

1. Job considered God sovereign.

For such a barrage of tragedy to strike so unexpectedly is uncommon. Job had some common and understandable reactions. What did Job do that you would consider unusual?

Job 1:20 – _____

_____

_____

In your own words, describe the attitude Job had toward God.

Job 1:21-22 – _____

_____

_____

When Job was physically afflicted, his wife advised him to curse God and die. What was his response?

"'You speak as _____ speaks.

Shall we indeed _____ and

not _____?' In all

this Job _____" (Job 2:10).

2. Job considered God unfair.

Job did not understand why such calamity surrounded his life. He felt he had done nothing against God to deserve such treatment. How did Job believe God felt toward him?

110

The very circumstances Job questioned gave him purpose, destiny, and insight to life.

2. Job accepted God's ways.

God again spoke through Elihu. What insight about God's doings did he explain to Job?

"God thunders His voice _____, doing_____

_____" (Job 37:5).

Because Job didn't understand God's purpose, he questioned God's ways. He later realized God knew exactly what He was doing.

What did Job confess he did not know?

"'Who is this that hides counsel without knowledge?' Therefore I have

declared _____

_____, things _____

_____, which I did not know" (Job 42:3).

Job accepted the means God used to accomplish His purpose. Job's entire outlook on tragic circumstances changed. His suffering and loss wasn't less, he simply accepted, by faith, God's way as best.

Job's circumstances changed drastically. God blessed him with two times what he had before. Job died a wealthy, fulfilled man.

III. Steps to understanding God's purpose.

1. Focus on God rather than circumstances.

In summary, here are the four qualities of God we have been studying together, each joined with a Psalm praising God for that quality. Take the step of focusing on God's character rather than circumstances.

(1) Thank God for being your authority, protecting and providing for you.

"The Lord is near to all who call upon Him, to all who call upon

Him in truth. He will _____

_____; He will also _____

_____

_____. The Lord _____

_____; but all the wicked, He will destroy" (Psalm 145:18-20).

(2) Thank God for being all knowing.

"Thou dost know _____ and _____

_____; Thou dost understand _____

_____. Thou dost scrutinize _____

_____, and art intimately acquainted _____

_____. Even before there is a word on my

tongue, _____

_____" (Psalm 139:2-4).

(3) Thank God for being your strength.

"But as for me, _____; yes, I shall

joyfully sing of Thy lovingkindness in the morning, for Thou _____

_____, and _____

_____. O_____, I will sing praises to Thee;

for God is _____, the God who

shows me lovingkindness" (Psalm 59:16-17).

(4) Thank God for being in complete control.

"For I know that the Lord _____, and that our Lord is

above all gods. Whatever the Lord_____,

He _____, in _____, in the

_____" (Psalm 135:5-6).

2. Submit your circumstances to God's control.

Praising God for what and who He is conditions the heart and mind to act. Proper thining leads to proper action.

When I believe God is my provision, is all knowing, is my strength and has everything in His control, I must act upon that belief. If God is truly in control, my plans, ambitiions and will must be submitted to His will. All of life, both present and future, are to be submitted to His controlling will.

How much control do we have over our life?

"Yet _____

_____. You are just a vapor that _____

_____" (James 4:14).

"Instead, you ought to say, '_____, _____

_____'" (James 4:15).

3. Believe God is accomplishing His purpose.

There are three things to keep in mind as our faith is tested.

(1) God will not allow more than we can endure.

"No temptation has overtaken you but such as is _____

_____; and God is faithful, _____

_____

but with the temptation _____,

that _____

_____" (1 Corinthians 10:13).

(2) God is at work in us.

"For it is _____, both

_____" (Philippians 2:13).

(3) God is making us like Christ.

"And we know that _____

_____ to those who love God, to those who are called according

to His purpose. For whom He foreknew, He also _____

_____, that He might be the firstborn among many brethren"
(Romans 8:28-29).

Conclusion

God demonstrated His control through the life of Job. God's purpose was not altered by tragic circumstances. God was in complete control, using each situation to bring about His purpose. The experience of Job confirms that God is worthy of our trust. When we place our trust in God's control, it gives a sense of purpose.

———————O———————

Feedback

Agree or disagree (mark A or D)

_____1. God's purpose was fulfilled through Job's life, even though Job didn't know what it was.

_____2. When trying circumstances come, the best thing to do is focus on the reason for the problem.

_____3. Focusing on God's character gives us a basis for our trust.

_____4. God's purpose in us is accomplished by our taking charge and doing our best to control our lives.

———————O———————

My Response

Josh

Knowing God as controller helps me understand myself better. My ambitions and plans become apparent. Some Christians submit their plans to God until they have no ambition or plans for life. Others develop extensive goals and ask God to merely agree with them. Neither of these extremes is correct. First, I make plans in the area that God has gifted me. Second, I make sure those plans honor the name of Jesus Christ. And last, I try to be sensitive to the alteration of those plans by the Holy Spirit. In this way, my ambitions and plans are not diminished, and I become more ambitious for Christ. I rejoice in the fact that He is in control.

_____

(My name)

In what area of my life do I sense my faith being tested regarding God's control?

_____

_____

_____

What are some Christlike attitudes I am to exhibit during this trying time?

_____

_____

_____

To reinforce my trust in God's control, I will pray:

"Lord Jesus, I know You have a specific purpose for me and my life. I thank You for each circumstance You bring me into because I know You are teaching me something about Yourself. Help me to know You better through these difficult times. I place my trust in Your ability to work all things for my good and Your glory. Amen."

GLOSSARY

APOLOGETICS: A defense of the truth. In Christian doctrine, it is a logical presentation of reasons and facts that show Christianity is the true and only religion of God. EV/1

CHRISTIAN EVIDENCES: The facts and truths of history, science and personal experience that substantiate the validity of the Christian faith. A sub-division of Christian apologetics. EV/1

DOCUMENTARY HYPOTHESIS: A theory which teaches that the Pentateuch was not authored by Moses, but was the result of a process of writing, re-writing, editing, and compiling by various anonymous editors years after Moses. MEV/29

EXTANT MANUSCRIPTS: The handwritten copies of original documents that have survived the centuries and are available for first hand examination and comparison. EV/40

FORM CRITICISM: A New Testament literary study of the method in which various "forms" of gospel tradition were passed on and eventually recorded as a series of disconnected stories and teachings unhistorically and artificially strung together. Translated from a German word meaning literally "history of form." MEV/183

HIGHER CRITICISM/CRITICS: A division of the science of biblical literary investigation which scrutinizes the books of the Bible to determine their age, authorship and mode of composition. MEV/35

MANUSCRIPT: Handwritten copy of an original document. EV/46

MANUSCRIPT ATTESTATION: A comparison of the number of existing manuscripts, together with the interval between the time written and the earliest copy, establishing a document's accuracy of transmission. EV/39

MASORETIC TEXT: The Old Testament Hebrew text, copied by highly disciplined scribes (the Masoretes), who standardized the Hebrew text by adding vowel points to insure proper pronunciation. From *Massora* "Tradition." EV/54

TEXTUAL CRITICISM: The general science of literary study to determine the historical reliability, accurate transmission and specific wording of ancient writings. MEV/35

WORLD VIEW: A comprehensive conception of human existence from a specific standpoint. The framework in which a person interprets reality. MEV/3

Reference Key:
   EV – *Evidence That Demands a Verdict*

   MEV – *More Evidence That Demands a Verdict*
         (Example: EV/1. EV means Evidence That Demands a Verdict;
         /1 means the page in the book that discusses that subject.)